How to Cope When the Money
Runs Out

How to Cope
When the Money
Runs Out

a handbook for survival by

David Benedictus

CANONGATE

First Published in Great Britain in 1998
by Canongate Books Ltd,
14 High Street, Edinburgh EH1 1TE

ISBN 0 86241 733 3

British Library Cataloguing-in-Publication Data
A catalogue record is available on request
from the British Library

Typeset by Palimpsest Book Production
Polmont, Stirlingshire

Printed and bound by
Caledonian International Book Manufacturing,
Bishopbriggs, Scotland

To those who don't believe that they can cope
any more. May they find that they can.

CONTENTS

Introduction

I don't know who you are or how serious your situation is. You may have been head of a mighty empire and now worry that they are about to cut off your electricity. It happens. You may never have had money, and that tiny air bubble which kept you afloat all those years may have popped through circumstances quite beyond your control. Perhaps you are still just about all right, but living on your diminishing capital has got you so worried that you are determined to take action before it is too late.

All I do know about you is that you are reading – and may even have bought – this book. So I shall assume that you belong to that freemasonry of have-nots to whom the travel pages of the papers are a slap in the face, and the endless advertisements for expensive toys at Christmas remind you distressingly that your friends and family who deserve so much will receive so little. And children – that is where the pain is greatest; to see them denied what other children have as of right, well, that won't do at all. Let me try and help you at least with that.

A few home truths are necessary here. There is nothing shameful about poverty. It is no exaggeration to say that almost all our greatest artists, writers and composers have endured it. It is not particularly helpful – though interesting – to speculate that they might not have been so great had they not had to endure it.

Nor is it always shameful if it is your own silly fault that you have become poor. We are told that we live in 'an enterprise economy', which is good news if you are a born entrepreneur. Not everybody is. When I hear that phrase I sometimes wonder what it would have been like to have lived in a sweet-tooth economy, or a red-hair economy, or a tall economy – your income increased by a thousand a year for every centimetre above the norm.

This book is a guiding hand through that enterprise economy, a torch to pierce the gloom and enable you to find the ladders and avoid the snakes. How to cope when the money runs out and retain your self-respect. Once the bills are all paid, you may even be surprised at how straightforward it all was.

In the early preparation of this book I spoke to the Samaritans and invited them to share with me some of the most frequently encountered anxieties. They preferred not to, being very discreet people, and needfully so. So when I suggested that my book would advise people to remember that There Are Always Others Worse Off Than Yourself, they stated categorically that this was the worst remark one could possibly make. Nonetheless, I believe it to be some comfort to remember that, if you can't pay the mortgage this month, there are those who are six months behind with their mortgage. *You* are six months behind with your mortgage? Consider those whose homes are already being repossessed.

There are numerous booklets published by well-meaning authorities and charities to help people who have got in over their heads. Some of them offer specific advice with

a born entrepreneur

helpful charts and formulae. Many of these are useful and I have listed some at the end of this book. There is also a plethora of helplines, Citizens Advice Bureaux, and trained debt counsellors to whom you can turn; these too I have detailed.

It is not my intention to duplicate the advice you can get elsewhere, but to set out the most practical advice in a sensible sort of way, and to recommend what you ought to do next in the circumstances in which you find yourself.

When you find it hard to eat or sleep, when you hear yourself lying to friends and relations, even to yourself, that is the moment to remind yourself: *my problems are practical, and it must therefore be possible to apply practical solutions to them.*

1.   The Awful Truth (Part One)

Last year at this time Caitlin and I were doing an act in a garret. This time we're just as poor, or poorer, but the ravens – soft, white, silly ravens – will feed us.

from a letter by Dylan Thomas (1938)

A common form of self-deception is to believe you are being honest with yourself, and then to leave out some vital piece of evidence. It is the equivalent of an alcoholic pouring down the sink the six bottles of vodka he had hidden in the coal-cellar, while ignoring the bottle which is even more securely hidden behind the fridge.

But there are signs which simply cannot be ignored.

1. There never seems to be any money in the bank account. You can't understand this. You seem to be paying more in than you are withdrawing, and yet the figures get worse and worse. You settle down with the statement, vowing to go through it carefully, to establish just how it is that the bank keeps making these mistakes, and why it is that the mistakes always seem to be in the bank's favour. Half an hour later you reach for the packet of fags. Crikey! The bank has not been making mistakes. You had failed to

take into account that direct debit you signed which was supposed to make things easier, the interest on the overdraft, the cheque you gave your sister to tide you over the week-end when you found yourself 'temporarily embarrassed' (a comforting phrase implying that the condition will right itself, and that you are not accustomed to such things).

2. You find cheques being returned 'please re-present' or even 'refer to drawer'. What is worse, each time this happens you find a hefty charge – probably £25 – being debited to your account.

3. You put your cash card into the dispenser, and instead of that encouraging whirring sound, a message appears on the screen, advising you to take the matter up with your bank. You try to ignore the

smirk on the face of the person behind you in the queue.

4. It seems ridiculous but every so often, and it's more often than it used to be, you find yourself with *absolutely no money at all*. Of course it's ridiculous and next Tuesday things will be fine again, but just for the moment . . . It so happens that this is the day when your eight-year-old reminds you that she has to take in her dinner money. So what do you propose to say to her, and what do you recommend she says to the dinner lady?

5. You have stopped opening all the brown envelopes, and even a few of the more ominous-looking white ones, that come flooding through the door. You certainly check the postmark to see if you can identify from whom they might be before deciding whether or not to open them. You keep saying: 'No need to deal with that one now. I'll deal with them all together when I have a good clear-out at the weekend.'

6. Since last Thursday when the knock at the door proved to be the electricity man wanting a cheque to pay the outstanding bill or else they would be obliged to disconnect, you have been alarmed by knocks at the door, and relieved when they turn out to be Doctor Barnardo or the Lib Dems. You raised the matter of the electricity bill with your spouse whom you thought was responsible for paying the bills. He/she claimed that she/he had paid it, or thought that he/she had. You ask: what about the gas? telephone? water? community charge? Even though the response may be reassuring, there is

an evasiveness in the way in which that response is delivered which cannot be ignored.

7. Due to these niggling problems you decide to postpone that visit to the hairdressers, which you had promised yourself. That day trip to Paris through the Tunnel, which had seemed such a brilliant bargain when you read about it in the paper (and tore the advertisement out and left it pinned to the noticeboard so that you wouldn't forget) now seems a dubious enterprise. Suppose you arrive in Paris and you've only got enough money for an Evian Water? Where's the fun in that?

8. You suddenly realise that it's only twenty-three shopping days to Christmas, and you haven't started buying the food or the presents. If only you can pay the minimum on the credit card, you'll be able to use that, of course, but what about the increased minimum you will have to pay in January? And if you can't pay that, will you even be able to attend the January sales, a treat you have come to rely upon? Oh lord, but there's a good chance something will turn up to relieve the pressure in January. (Something will turn up in January, but it won't relieve the pressure. January is the month when the bank shoves on the interest charges for the previous year's borrowing. Had you thought of that, my friend?)

9. Your eye keeps being seduced by these ads on the television, in the bank, in the newspapers, offering to lend you money at such brilliant terms, that it seems almost as if they are paying you to borrow money from them.

10. For the first time since that dreadful row with your

mother you find your appetite has gone. You sit for five minutes in front of the cornflakes, and finally give them to the cat (who doesn't want them either). You wonder if there is a connection between what the postman brought and this unusual loss of appetite. Come to think of it, you haven't been sleeping too well either. Come to think of it, could there be a connection between all this and the fact that you/your spouse couldn't get it up/has had a 'bit of a headache' so frequently recently?

If you recognise five or more of these symptoms it is horribly clear that you need to make lists.

If you know that you cannot pay many of the bills that is no excuse not to pay any of the bills. The critical question is which to prioritise, how much to pay, and what to do about the others.

Let us take a seemingly straightforward case. You work at a travel agency. You are a widow with two children, a boy of twelve and a girl of ten. They are being educated at the local comprehensive. It is October 12th. You have a bank overdraft of £800, which is a reducing overdraft, that is to say it has been agreed that you will reduce it by £50 a month.

You look at your last bank statement and discover that you have already spent £375 of that £800.

Is there any good news?

Your monthly pay cheque of £1850 is due on the 20th. Your widowed mother's allowance is £61.15 a week plus £9.90 for the first child and £11.15 for the second. Then there is child benefit at £10.80 a week for Geoffrey and £8.80 a week for Stephanie.

Within the next month you can therefore expect to receive:

	£
Pay cheque	1850.00
Widowed mother's allowance	244.60
for Geoffrey	39.60
for Stephanie	44.60
Children's allowances	
for Geoffrey	43.20
for Stephanie	35.20
Lottery win	Don't be silly
Total	2257.20

You have a standing order of £30 per month for life insurance. This is paid by direct debit on the 20th as is your mortgage, at £575 per month.

You have £425 (£800–£375) to spend between now and the 20th. On the 20th you will have £425 plus £1850 = £2275. Add the allowances and benefits and you come up with an additional £407.20, making £2682.20. But this will have to be reduced by £50 (reducing overdraft) + £30 (life insurance) + £575 (mortgage). Therefore between the 20th October and the 20th November, you will have £2682.20 less £655, which comes to £2027.20, and a reducing £750 overdraft.

Now, steeling yourself with a strong cup of coffee, you bring out the sheaf of unpaid bills. With mounting horror you discover that you owe:

	£
The tax man (for the previous financial year)	800.00
(for this financial year)	1780.00

	£
The gas man	248.00
The electricity company	158.00
Water rates	87.00
Visa card	
(minimum payment required – £44)	879.00
Access card	
(minimum payment required – £54)	1067.00
Amex card	
(full settlement required each month)	680.00
Phone bill	279.00
Total	5978.00

Making yourself an even stronger cup of coffee, and wondering why they always seem so calm when they drink coffee in the advertisements, you realise that there is more, much more.

It is your son, Geoffrey's, birthday on the 15th, and you have promised to take him and his six best friends to the cinema and the local McDonalds. Stephanie, your daughter, will have to come along too, of course. You have not yet bought Geoffrey a present, and he is desperate for a pair of trainers, which you inadvertently promised him.

You have been invited out to a meal on the 23rd by a friend of your late husband's who is your daughter's godfather. It is important to keep in well with him. At the moment the children are old enough to look after themselves for a couple of hours when they get back from school and before you get home from work. But you can't leave them alone for a whole evening. You will need a baby-sitter. Plus you will have to have your one decent dress dry-cleaned for the dinner, although you'll just have to do the best you can with your hair.

The old Renault has its MOT early next month, and that ominous rattle in the suspension means all may not be well.

You need to make a supplementary list as follows:

	£
Nine cinema tickets	31.50
Nine Mcdonalds meals	45.00
Pair of trainers	50.00
Baby-sitter	15.00
Dry-cleaning	8.00
MOT	28.00
Suspension (educated guess)	200.00
Total	377.50

To sum up your circumstances, therefore:

	£
Money to spend for the next month	2027.20
Domestic expenditure for the next month	377.50
Owed	5978.00

You realise quickly enough that this is by no means the complete picture. But for the moment you have to sort out the necessities. And the best thing to appreciate is a great truth, which is almost certainly in the Talmud, i.e. some debts are more necessitous than others.

The electricity company's bill is in fact a reminder that they will disconnect the supply on Wednesday if they have not received settlement. The Amex card is also abrupt. If they do not receive payment of the full amount they will be required to close your account. This will be particularly inconvenient because your work for the travel agents requires you to travel from time to time, and you have a corporate American Express card. The phone bill is also horribly red.

But you only have £425 to spend in the next eight days.

a) You must pay the electricity bill – £158
b) You must buy a present for your son, and pay for his party – £126.50
c) Maybe you can pay the minimum on your Visa and Access cards – £98

That will leave you just £42.50 for emergencies. And what about the Amex card? And the tax man?

You conclude that you are in fact getting nowhere. Your big bills are not reducing. Indeed they seem to be increasing since there is interest to be paid on them as well. You decide that you will draw up a better list, one that will include everything. One that will give you some idea of how you are likely to be positioned over the coming twelve months, rather than the coming thirty days. Excellent. And you decide that, in order not to get too depressed, you will get the bad news out of the way first, and concentrate on outgoings before incomings.

This is what your better list should look like. (I have left it to you to fill in the figures.) Only some of the categories will apply to you, thank goodness.

OUTGOINGS

1. Weekly

a) Rent
b) Food

c) School meals
d) Pocket money
e) Lottery
f) Pet food
g) House cleaning
h) Newspapers and magazines
i) Laundry
j) Dry cleaning
k) Babysitter
l) Booze
m) Fags
n) Entertainment (theatre, cinema, videos, concerts, clubs, books, audio books)
o) Sports or hobbies
p) Any other gambling habits

The following (q–u) may be paid by purchasing a weekly stamp from the Post Office. This takes the misery out of the big quarterly bills, and is therefore a Good Idea.

q) TV licence
r) Gas
s) Electricity
t) Road fund (but see also 5k below)
u) Telephone bill

2. *Monthly*

a) Mortgage
b) Second mortgage
c) Allowances for children at college
d) Car running costs, including petrol and oil
e) Prescriptions, dentist, optician etc

f) Clothes
g) Children's clothes
h) Working clothes, equipment, stationery etc.
i) Books
j) Fuel costs (besides gas and electricity i.e. oil, solid fuel)
k) Other school expenses (besides food)
l) TV rental
m) Sky TV subscription

3. *Quarterly*

a) VAT (if you are registered)
b) Water rates
c) Accountant

4. *Three Times a Year*

a) School fees

5. *Annual*

a) Ground rent
b) Council tax
c) Income tax (if not PAYE)
d) Life insurance
e) House insurance
f) Contents insurance
g) Repairs to house/ redecorations
h) Presents
i) Christmas
j) Holidays (travel, hotel, special clothes, spending money)
k) Road Fund licence (or twice yearly)

l) MOT

m) Car repairs and servicing

n) Car insurance (some brokers permit monthly payments)

o) Depreciation of value of car

p) Membership of AA, RAC etc.

q) Subscriptions to clubs, union dues etc.

r) Charities

s) Plants etc for garden

t) Gardener

u) Vet's fees

v) Any savings plans, including TESSAs, PEPs and suchlike

w) Bank interest and charges

x) Anything else you can think of

Some of these you will have to estimate, and some of these you will have to average out, but have a go anyway.

This list should give you a clear picture – perhaps depressingly clear – of how much your outgoings may be per week, per month, per quarter and per year. Once you have completed it, you should be able to check each item to discover whether there is any way in which that one can be reduced, or eliminated altogether. Often there is.

A useful trick is to fill in the same form for last year's expenditure and an estimated one for next year's expenditure. Are you tightening your belt or letting it out a notch? Be honest.

Now for the good news. When you work out your

incomings, although the list is a good deal shorter than the outgoings, it can be greater than you think.

INCOMINGS

1. *Weekly*

   a) Wages
   b) Overtime (guaranteed)
   c) Overtime (sporadic – an educated guess)
   d) 2nd earner wages
   e) 2nd earner overtime (guaranteed)
   f) 2nd earner overtime (sporadic – an educated guess)
   g) Rent from lodger
   h) Pension
   i) Other benefits – see next chapter
   j) Moonlighting (net profit)

2. *Monthly*

   a) Salary
   b) Pension
   c) Benefits – see next chapter

3. *Twice Yearly*

   a) Dividends (an educated guess)

4. *Annual*

   a) Anything else you can think of

Benefits. These are so numerous, so complicated, and such a minefield that I thought it sensible to devote a whole chapter to them. But don't go away. We shall return to your personal circumstances after a very boring, but necessary chapter.

2.   You Mean I Get All That? No!

I've got no money for Christmas presents. But I have made my Christmas list in case I find ten pounds in the street.

from *The Secret Diary of Adrian Mole aged 13¾*
by Sue Townsend

This is a *boring* chapter. Unavoidable. But I suggest you glance down the left hand column, arranged in user-friendly alphabetical order, to check which (if any) relate to your circumstances, and ignore the rest.

I have listed every way in which our enlightened government currently (February 1998) gives us money, or returns to us some of the money we have given it. As you will see, you need to have a doctorate of philosophy to understand the full implications of all these grants, allowances and awards. I have put in brackets after the entries the number of the pamphlet issued by the Benefits Agency – the loving and caring branch of the Social Security Department – which sets out full details of what you are entitled to under each category and how to apply.

These leaflets are available at Social Security Offices, at Citizens Advice Bureaux, at your local Council Offices (for Housing Benefit and Council Tax matters), at NHS hospitals, doctors, dentists, opticians and pharmacists (for health cost documents), from public libraries and from some Post Offices and Jobcentres. They are all free.

So when you've decided which benefits you might be entitled to, send off for the leaflets relating to them.

If your first language is not English – you'll have done well to get this far in my book! – advice on benefits is available in Arabic, Bengali, Chinese, Greek, Gujarati, Hindi, Punjabi, Somali, Turkish, Urdu and Vietnamese. Ask for Leaflet **FB 22** in the language of your choice. If there are any Welsh speakers out there who don't speak English they will need to apply for **FB2 Wales**. If you're a Gaelic speaker, tough.

If you are still puzzled a quick route is to look up BENEFITS AGENCY, CONTRIBUTIONS AGENCY (for National Insurance matters), or SOCIAL SECURITY in the phone book, and give them a buzz.

The Benefits Agency runs a confidential telephone service for those with disabilities and those who care for them. Try 0800 88 22 00 for general – but not personalised – advice. And of course you can always visit your local Citizens Advice Bureau, which ought to be able to point you in the right direction.

The Benefit rates given here were valid from April 1997. The codes in brackets after each entry refer to the numbers of the relevant leaflet(s).

ATTENDANCE ALLOWANCE (AA)

A tax-free weekly cash payment for those sixty-five and over who need personal care because of an illness or disability. The good news is that it's not dependent on National Insurance contributions, that it's in no way means tested, and that it shouldn't affect any Income Support or Jobseeker's Allowance claims.

You must have been in need of help for six months or more, but it doesn't matter whether you're getting the help or not. All that matters is that you need it.

Now it becomes a touch surreal. If you are not expected to live more than six months there are special rules for you which mean that you get the top rate straight away, and that the officials give your case top priority. If you then *don't* die when you were meant to, they can't grab the money back, so it's one in the eye for the benefits officials as well as the doctors! The higher rate is £49.50 (if you need help day *and* night); the lower rate is £33.10 (if you need help day *or* night).

(DS 702)

BACK TO WORK BONUS

If you have been entitled to Income Support or Job-seeker's Allowance for at least ninety-one days and if you work part-time, you could be entitled to a Back To Work Bonus, a cash lump sum of up to £1000 which you can claim when your benefit stops, subject to the number of hours you work, or the amount you earn.

(WWB 11)

BUDGETING LOANS

Interest-free but repayable, these can help with necessary but expensive items, such as beds or cookers, or with removals or repairs. You will probably need to have been receiving Income Support or a Jobseeker's Allowance for at least twenty-six weeks.

(SF 300)

CHILD BENEFITS

A tax-free weekly benefit for everyone who is responsible for a child aged under sixteen, or under eighteen if the child is still receiving full-time education up to GCE A Level (Highers in Scotland). (In this case it continues until the end of the holidays following the term in which your child has completed its education.) Currently the benefit stands at a modest £11.05 a week for the first child (£17.10 if you are a lone parent) and £9 for subsequent children.

(CH 1, CH 8 and **FB 8)**

CHILD MAINTENANCE

This is the same as Child Support. Child Maintenance is a controversial initiative run by the Child Support Agency, wittily known as the CSA. Unless the agency considers that there is a risk of harm or distress to you or your children resulting from applying, you may be *required* to apply for maintenance if you or your present partner are currently receiving Income Support, Jobseeker's Allowance, Family Credit, or Disability Working Allowance. If you are an Absent Parent you may also qualify for maintenance for the child. Whether or not you may apply for this or must wait to be approached by the CSA is currently unclear. If you are a little confused about the operation of this scheme – and you wouldn't be human if you are not – try ringing the Enquiry Line on 0345 133 133 between 9 a.m. and 5 p.m.

(CSA 2001)

CHILD SUPPORT

This is the same as Child Maintenance, except that it is sometimes known officially as Child Support Maintenance. Whatever.

CHRISTMAS BONUS

This tax-free bonus comes automatically or as a separate payment during the first week in December, if you're in receipt of benefit. It's only a tenner, so it may just about pay for a box of crackers or a smallish turkey.

COLD WEATHER PAYMENT

If you or your partner are already getting Income Support, or Jobseeker's Allowance, you *may* qualify for one of these. If you do, the money will be sent to you automatically (no need to make a claim). When do you get one? Only if the average temperature for seven days in a row is, or is forecast to be, freezing point or below. Attempts to include the wind-chill factor in the equation have, so far, failed. A well-meaning but dotty benefit costing, I suspect, far more to administer than it's worth. The weekly payment is £8.50.

(CWP 1)

COMMUNITY CARE GRANTS

You will probably need to be in receipt of Income Support and/or Jobseeker's Allowance to qualify for one of these. They are intended to help people in special circumstances (elderly and disabled for instance) and those leaving institutions or residential care who may need help in adjusting to community life. The grants are not loans and do not have to be paid back.

(SF 300)

COUNCIL TAX BENEFIT
(if you pay Council Tax)

Generally speaking if you qualify for Housing Benefit, you also qualify for Council Tax Benefit, which will help you to pay the Council Tax. There is a maximum of 100% benefit which means that if your circumstances are serious enough you should not have to pay any Council Tax at all.

You can claim this benefit at the same time as claiming Income Support or Jobseeker's Allowance.

Deductions for non-dependants are at the upper rate (gross income £114 or more per week – £2.60); or the lower rate (gross income less than £114 per week – £1.30).

(CTB 1)

CRISIS LOANS

You may get one of these after an emergency, crisis or disaster which may pose a serious risk to yourself or your family. It will usually look after you over a fourteen-day period, but although it's interest free, it's repayable. You qualify even if you're not in receipt of any other benefit.

(SFL 2 and **SB 16)**

DISABILITY LIVING ALLOWANCE (DLA)

A tax-free benefit for people who need help with personal care, with getting about, or with both. It only applies to you if you're under sixty-five when you begin to need help. If you're older than that see Attendance Allowance. There are two parts to it, a care component, and a mobility component.

As with the Attendance Allowance it doesn't matter about your National Insurance contributions, and is not affected by savings or income enjoyed by yourself or your partner. Nor should it affect your Income Support or Jobseeker's Allowance claims.

To qualify you must have been in need of help for at least three months, and be likely to need it for at least another six. If your illness is thought to be terminal you will qualify for special rules (see Attendance Allowance).

	Care component	Mobility component
	£	£
Highest rate	49.50	34.60
Middle rate	33.10	–
Lowest rate	13.15	13.15

The Benefit Inquiry Line 0800 882200 is available for people with disabilities and their carers.

(HB 6 and **DS 704)**

DISABILITY WORKING ALLOWANCE

A tax-free income-related benefit. You will qualify if you're at least sixteen, and if you're working at least sixteen hours a week on average, and if you're ill or disabled, making it difficult for you to look for a job. Your National Insurance contributions are not taken into account.

The bad news is that you don't qualify if for the previous fifty-six days you haven't been receiving a disability benefit, or if you're on a training scheme receiving a training allowance.

You must be already in receipt of one of these: DLA *or* Attendance Allowance *or* various war disablement *or* industrial injuries benefits. The amount is variable.

There is a good deal of small print on this one and you need to read very carefully leaflets **HB 4** and/or **DS 703** – obtainable from the usual places (see beginning of chapter).

Adult Allowance

Single £49.55   Couple/Lone Parent £77.55

EDUCATIONAL MAINTENANCE AWARDS

These are means tested awards to young people at school after leaving age and are made at the discretion of the local council. Ask at the town hall, city chambers or education department.

FAMILY CREDIT

A tax-free benefit for working families with children. It does not depend on National Insurance contributions, is not a loan, and does not, therefore, have to be paid back.

The amount depends on how many children you have,
what their ages are, your family income, any savings, the
amount of childcare charges you pay, and the number of
hours you work.

	£
Adult credit (one parent or a couple)	47.45
30-hour credit (a parent working 30 hours or more a week)	10.55
Additionally for each child under 11	12.05
For each child of 11–15	19.95
For each child of 16–17	24.80
For each child of 18	34.70

(FB 4, FC 1 or telephone 0800 500 222, or for fuller details
01253 50 00 50**)**

FUNERAL PAYMENT

When a family member dies, this is activated. You or your
partner must be in receipt of one of the major benefits to
qualify. Up to £600 can be awarded for the funeral costs,
plus whatever's necessary for a burial or cremation. The
money is repayable out of the deceased's estate.

(SF 200)

HOUSING BENEFIT (PAID TO TENANTS ONLY)

Paid by local councils if you need help in paying your
rent. What it is *not* for is mortgage interest payments,
fuel costs, meals, and some service charges. You won't
get Housing Benefit if you and your partner jointly have
over £16,000 in savings.

A complicated equation applies, involving deductions for non-dependants, allowances for single people under twenty-five and lone parents under eighteen, a premium for all lone parents, meal deductions for adults and children, and fuel charge deductions. But you may be entitled to 100% of your eligible rent. If you're puzzled – as you might well be – you can ask the Citizens Advice Bureau to guide you through the minefield. They won't mind.

(RR 1)

INCAPACITY BENEFIT

This is for you if you're under state pension age and if illness or disability makes it impossible for you to work. It is very complicated and you should refer to the appropriate leaflets to find out how much you may be entitled to, and how it may most conveniently be paid.

Short-term Incapacity Benefit

	£
Higher rate	55.70 per week
Lower rate	47.10 per week

Long-term Incapacity Benefit

Basic rate	62.45 per week

(IB 201 and 202)

INCOME SUPPORT

A Social Security benefit for people aged sixteen and over whose annual income (jointly with a partner or alone) is below £8000 *and* who is not working more than sixteen hours a week *and* who does not have a partner who works twenty-four hours or more per week on average, *and* who is not required to be available for work because he/she is sick or disabled, a lone parent or foster parent, sixty or over, getting Invalid Care Allowance for looking after someone.

You also must be habitually resident in the UK to qualify. In other words if you haven't much money, and can't do full-time work for a very good reason, you ought to be all right.

The good news is that you can get this benefit even if you haven't been paying your National Insurance contributions. And it can be paid to you to top up earnings from part-time and/or self-employed work, or if you've got nothing at all coming in.

Complicated mathematics is involved so study the leaflets.

(FB 4, IS 1 Income Support. Or **IS 20** for full details)

INDUSTRIAL INJURIES DISABLEMENT BENEFIT

This is for you if you have been unfortunate enough to have been injured at work. It may be paid in addition to Incapacity Benefit. How much you get depends, reasonably, on how badly you were injured. It's split into Reduced Earnings Allowance, Constant Attendance Allowance, and Exceptionally Severe Disablement Allowance. The highest rate is £101.10 per week; the lowest rate is £20.22 per week.

(**NI 2** (industrial disease), **NI 3** (pneumoconiosis or byssinosis), **NI 6** (industrial injuries disablement), **NI 7** (coal miners, bronchitis and emphysema), **NI 207** (deafness as a result of your job), **NI 237** (asthma as a result of your job), **NI 272** (asbestosis as a result of your job).

INVALID CARE ALLOWANCE (ICA)

You qualify for this if you're between sixteen and sixty-five, earning no more than £50 a week after deduction of allowable expenses, not in full-time education, and spending more than thirty-five hours a week caring for someone who is in receipt of Constant Attendance Allowance and/or Disability Living Allowance. This benefit does not depend on National Insurance contributions. ICA is £37.35 per week.

(DS 700)

JOBSEEKER'S ALLOWANCE (JSA)

This has replaced the old Unemployed Benefit and Income Support, as that related to unemployed job-seekers. A pack giving full details and a claims form is obtainable from any Jobcentre.

Briefly, you can get this useful allowance if you're capable of work, looking for work, and available for work; if you've paid enough National Insurance contributions and don't have much in the way of income or savings; if you're out of work, or working fewer than sixteen hours a week; or if your partner is out of work and working fewer than twenty-four hours a week; if you're at least eighteen and under state pensionable age; not in full-time education; a resident of the UK. There are some circumstances when you might get a JSA if you're sixteen or seventeen, but I wouldn't count on it. And there may be problems if you're on a training scheme, since you won't then be available for work until the training is completed. Tricky!

The rates paid depend on a number of variables. If, for example, you have no income but your partner works 10 hours a week, earning £30 and you have no children, you would get £49.15.

(NI 196, JSA L5)

MATERNITY ALLOWANCE

A national insurance benefit payable for eighteen weeks (if you haven't fallen behind with your National Insurance payments) for those who don't get a Maternity Benefit from their company.

(FB 8)

If you're unemployed, or self-employed when you qualify, you get £48.35. If you're employed when you qualify, you get £55.70.

(NI 17a, FB 8)

MATERNITY PAYMENT (SOCIAL FUND)

If you are about to have or have just had a baby, you may be entitled to one of these. It's worth £100 to help towards the costs of a new baby. See also Statutory Maternity Pay.

(SF 100)

MONEY IN LIEU OF NOTICE

You may qualify if you've been sacked or made redundant and can't for any reason work out your period of notice. Have a word with your Citizens Advice Bureau. In severe cases an industrial tribunal may be your only recourse. See Redundancy Payments.

NHS PRESCRIPTIONS

You can get these free if you're under sixteen (or under nineteen if you're a full-time student); if you're receiving Disability Working Allowance, Income Support, income-based Jobseeker's Allowance or Family Credit; if you're pregnant or have had a baby during the last year; if you're over sixty; if you're getting a war or disability pension and you need medicines for the disability you get the pension for; or if you suffer from one of the conditions listed in **HC 11**.

Free dental treatment and sight tests, help with the costs of glasses and contact lenses, NHS wigs and hearing aids, spinal and abdominal supports or surgical brassieres, hospital travel costs, and free medicines if you have to stay in hospital, generally require the same kind of qualifications.

(**HC 1, HC 11** (and **FL 11** for foreign language speakers))

LONE PARENT BENEFIT

This replaced the former One Parent Benefit in April 1997. Splendidly straightforward. If you're bringing up a child on your own you're entitled to a tax-free weekly

benefit on top of Child Benefit. It doesn't matter whether
or not you are the child's parent. There is one drawback.
If you're living with someone 'as if you are married to
them', no dice. The benefit is paid to the first or oldest
child only. If you're in a position to claim widows'
benefits instead you will probably do better to do so.
See entry under Child Benefit for the figures.

(CH 11 or FB 8)

REDUCED EARNINGS ALLOWANCE

If, as a result of an accident or a disabling sickness
which took place before the 1st October, 1990, you can't
return to your regular occupation or 'do work of the
same standard' (whatever that means), you qualify for
this.

You will only receive it beyond pensionable age, however, if you continue in regular employment after this
age.

(NI 6 and BI 103)

REDUNDANCY PAYMENTS

If you're made redundant and worked for your employer
for at least two years, you're entitled to some cash. If you
don't get it you must apply to an industrial tribunal. **But
if you don't do that within six months of being out of
work you will be too late!**

To find out more about these payments and how to
apply for them, contact your Citizens Advice Bureau.

You were self employed, you fired yourself, you received no redundancy payment and now you want to take yourself to an industrial tribunal?

RETIREMENT PENSION

This is the Big One. If you're a man of sixty-five, or a woman of sixty you will get this pension, the amount being based upon the National Insurance contributions you've made during your working life.

	£
Category A	
Basic pension (based on your own or late spouse's contributions):	62.45
Category B (married woman)	37.35
Category B (widow/widower)	62.45
Non-contributory:	
Full rate	37.35

(NP 46)

SECTION 17 PAYMENTS

These may be paid to stop a child being taken into care, if, for instance, fuel supplies are about to be disconnected, or an eviction order is being served. For details, phone your Citizens Advice Bureau.

SEVERE DISABLEMENT ALLOWANCE (SDA)

A tax-free benefit if, as a result of sickness or disablement, you haven't been able to work for at least twenty-eight consecutive weeks, but can't draw your Incapacity Benefit because insufficient NI contributions have been paid.

You must be between sixteen and sixty-five. And if you first became incapable of work after your twentieth birthday you will only qualify if you are assessed as at least 80% disabled. How much you get depends on how bad your disability is, and how old you were when you became unable to work. If you have children or dependants you could receive additional payments.

(SDA 1)

SOCIAL FUND

This is a camel (a horse designed by a committee). Part of it concerns payments towards maternity expenses (see Maternity Payment), cold weather expenses (see Cold Weather Payment), and the costs of a funeral (see Funeral Payment), and these are paid only if you can satisfy specific rules, which are at the discretion of the people running your local Benefits Agency, who will need to be persuaded that you receive Income Support, and that you don't have a nest egg tucked away under the mattress. 'At the discretion of' means that the decision of the agency may be appealed through review procedures, and reviewed again. You may challenge both the granting of the money, and the amount granted. Time-consuming though, and you would need to consider whether your time might not be better spent stuffing envelopes.

STATUTORY MATERNITY PAY

If you're in employment and pregnant you will be entitled to money from your company. This may be *statutory* (your company is required to pay you) if you've worked for them for more than nine months by the date the baby is expected; or *contractual* (should be in your conditions of employment) in which case it may be worth more – check your contract. The rate is £55.70 per week.

(NI 17a, FB 8)

STATUTORY SICK PAY (SSP)

This is for employed people. If you earn no less than £61 per week (the lowest earning limit for payment of Class 1 National Insurance), you should get SSP when you are off sick for four or more days in a row (including Sundays and Bank Holidays). The standard rate is £55.70.

(NI 244)

TAX ALLOWANCES

These aren't really benefits at all, just an entitlement to pay the government less than you otherwise might have to. Any changes to the rules are announced in the annual Budget, although they may take some time to be incorporated into the tax system. If you are a tax payer and have an accountant, make sure the accountant is fully apprised of any special circumstances which may qualify you for an allowance; if you do your own returns (I sympathise) you must make sure you are familiar with all the details. If you find that the tax inspector rejects some of your claimed allowances and expenses, you are allowed to argue your case. Details of the various allowances and so forth may be obtained from your tax office.

The additional personal allowances may be useful if you are bringing up sprog(s) on your own. There is a special leaflet called Income Tax and One Parent Families **(IR 92)** also obtainable from your tax office or PAYE enquiry office. At either of these offices they should advise you about the whole murky area of allowances.

TAX RELIEF

As above but specifically refers to those items which may be deducted from your taxable income because they are necessary in the course of doing your job, but not automatically deducted by your employer. You can include special clothes, heat, light, telephones, tools, buying and running a car, and so on. But you do need to include a covering letter and evidence with your tax return.

TRANSFER TAX ALLOWANCE

Complicated. This relates to a married man transferring
part or all of his tax allowance to his wife. You should
really take advice on all three tax headings, unless you are
a financial wizard, and, if you are a financial wizard, the
only reason you might have for reading this book would
be to review it.

WAR PENSIONS

Misleading. You don't have to have served in the armed
forces or to have been in a war to qualify for one of these
pensions. If you were injured or disabled as a result of
service as a member of HM Armed Forces; involvement
in the Polish Forces Under British Command 1939–45;
enemy action while you were a civilian or Civil Defence
Volunteer 1939–45; detention by the enemy; enemy action
while you were a member of the Auxiliary Services, a
merchant seaman or a coastguard, you may be eligible.

You do not qualify if you're still a serving member of
the forces. The details are complicated.

(WPA 1 and **WPA 9**; Helpline 01253 858 858)

WAR WIDOW'S PENSION
(also payable to widowers and children)

If you were married to or the child of someone who was
killed in the armed forces, or who died later as a result of
injuries sustained in the armed forces, you are entitled to
one of these pensions. The amount is dependent upon the
rank of the deceased, the age of the widow or widower,

and the amount of other related saving or savings. If your husband, wife, mother or father died as a result of injuries or illness *not* directly related to service in the forces, too bad.

A special payment of £52.80 per week (disregarded for means-tested benefits) is payable if your late spouse's service ended before 31st March 1973.

(WPA 1 and WPA 9)

WIDOW'S BENEFITS

If your late husband has paid enough Class 1, Class 2 or Class 3 National Insurance contributions, you may qualify for social security widow's benefits.

How much you're entitled to depends on how old you were when your husband died or when your Widowed Mother's Allowance (see Widow's Payment) stopped. The full rate is £62.45.

(WPA 1 and WPA 9, NP 45)

WIDOW'S PAYMENT

A tax-free lump sum payment for widows who are not yet sixty, and for those over sixty whose husbands were not getting Retirement Pension when they died. You may also qualify for Widowed Mother's Allowance or Widow's Pension (see below) from the date your husband died. The lump sum is £1000.

(NP 45)

WIDOW'S PENSION

A taxable weekly benefit for women of forty-five or over (forty or over if your husband died before the 11th April, 1988). It applies when your Widowed Mother's Allowance ends. You should receive, too, any entitlement inherited from your late husband's earnings-related pensions. It should be paid automatically but if you haven't had yours, and think you should have, tell the local Social Securities Office. The standard rate is £62.45, the same as the Widowed Mother's Allowance.

(NP 45)

WIDOWED MOTHER'S ALLOWANCE

A taxable weekly benefit for all widows who have at least one child for whom they receive Child Benefit (see above). If you're expecting a child by your late husband, by artificial insemination or by *in vitro* fertilisation, you also qualify.

Now it gets complicated.

If your husband died before the 11th April, 1988 and you have a child under nineteen living with you, you may be entitled to the allowance, even if you're *not* getting Child Benefit. It works out at a basic rate plus extra (this element is tax-free) for each child that you get benefit for from the date your husband died, and also for any earnings-related pension your husband had acquired.

The good news is that you should receive this £62.45 automatically.

(NP 45)

WORKMEN'S COMPENSATION
SUPPLEMENTATION

You should be entitled to this if, before the 5th July, 1948 you had an accident at work or contracted a disease as a result of your work. It is free of tax, and you may get extra money for dependants.

(WS 1)

A few important rules which apply to Jobseeker's Allowance, Income Support, Housing Benefit, Council Tax Benefit, Disability Working Allowance, and Family Credit follow.

For **Housing Benefit, Council Tax Benefit, Disability Working Allowance,** and the **entitlement to residential care homes** or **nursing homes**, the maximum capital you are allowed to have is £16,000. This includes the value of any property owned. For the entitlement to a residential care home or nursing home the amount ignored is £10,000. In these cases for each £250 between £10,000 and £16,000, £1 a week is taken into account.

For **Income-based Jobseeker's Allowance, Income Support** and **Family Credit**, the maximum capital you are allowed to have is £8000. In the case of these benefits, for each £250 between £3000 and £8000, £1 a week is taken into account.

Income Disregards is a vile term for those parts of your income which should not be included when your entitlement is worked out. See the leaflets **IS 20** (for Income Support), **RR 2** (for Housing Benefit and Council Tax Benefit), **NI 261** (for Family Credit), and **HB 4** (for Disability Working Allowance).

For subtenants, where **Jobseeker's Allowance, Income Support, Housing Benefit, Council Tax Benefit, Disability Working Allowance** and **Family Credit** are claimed there is an allowance for furnished or unfurnished accommodation of £4 per week, and an addition for heating of £9.20 per week.

All of this is as simple as I can make it, but is still complicated, and there are many more details, particularly in the tendentious areas of Earnings Rules and National Insurance Contributions Rates, which are outside the scope of this book – a cop out, I admit it! – but with which you really ought to be familiar. When in doubt phone the Benefits Agency Helpline. The number again is 0800 88 22 00.

And the best of British luck.

3.   The Awful Truth (Part Two)

Every ring of the doorbell gives me an electric shock as I never know what the postman or telegraph boy is going to bring in. And if it is bad news all the blame will fall on me.

from a letter from James Joyce to Harriet Shaw
Weaver, 1st May, 1935

You will remember that we left you in something of a dilemma, with bills to pay and no clear way of paying them. Let's recapitulate the figures, and do so in the expectation that, along with the Widowed Mother's and Children's Allowances, you may be entitled to some of the benefits included in the last chapter. However, even if you are able to disentangle the benefits to which you are entitled, it will take you a while to hold any of them in your hot little hand, and may not, therefore, solve any of your most urgent problems.

We left you owing £5978, made up in this way:

	£
Tax man:	
From previous financial year	800.00
and for this	1780.00
Gas man	248.00
Electricity	158.00
Water rate	87.00
Visa card (minimum payment required £44)	879.00

Access card (minimum payment required £54)   1067.00
Amex card (full settlement required each month)   680.00
Phone bill   279.00

You also had your son's birthday looming large.
Here is what you must do.

1.   Pay the electricity bill.
2.   Pay the minimum on your Visa and Access cards.
3.   Keep aside £130 for your son's present and party.
4.   Write a grovelling letter to Amex – being an Ameri-can company they are not very hot on irony – and ask them if they would allow you to defer full payment of your account, but that in the interim you will not, of course, be using your card. Wait to see what they propose by way of payment. Better that than making an offer to them. They may require you to return the card, at least in the short term.

With credit card payments (and most other bills) the worst thing to do is nothing. Once you get a black mark on your credit reference it may be very difficult to get rid of, and embarrassing to have to live with. On the other hand one can manage fine with just a Visa card and a cheque guarantee card – these may be the same bit of plastic anyway. In extremis you may decide to manage with just a bank guarantee card. It is not easy to manage just with cash, unless you are able to live on what you draw in cash benefits.

5.   Write to the taxman (taxperson?) and apologise for the delay, but reassure him/her that you will pay the £800 (the most urgent and long awaited payment out

of your next month's pay packet) after which you will reassess the position.

For some mysterious reason the Vatman – HM Customs and Excise – is a much tougher nut to crack than the Inland Revenue.

6. Put the gas bill in a highly visible position. Ditto the phone bill. Ditto the water bill. None of these will be cut off without a further warning.

7. Dry-cleaner and hairdresser for the party on the 23rd. Forget them. Do the best you can with your hand-washing and ironing (the frock not the hair). A baby-sitter you will need of course, but local teenagers revising for exams don't charge a fortune.

8. Enjoy Geoffrey's party, and the dinner.

It seems a useful general rule to take your children into your confidence about your financial circumstances, rather than trying to hide things from them. You may have valuable supporters in them, and they may be willing to make sacrifices to help. They may even volunteer to take on newspaper rounds, baby-sitting, Saturday morning shop assisting, or other part-time paid work to help out.

Let's be positive and assume that you have been able to deal with your immediate cash-flow problems in the way which I have outlined. I hope you have. Now you need to look at the medium-term problems, and this is where you need to be rigorous with yourself. Look at the worst prognosis. Do *not* assume that the grant application will succeed. Do *not* count on the half-promise from the false friend who said: 'Of course I'll pay you back just as soon as I'm in a position to.' Do *not* assume that you will win the Lottery next week. Indeed it is more sensible to stop buying tickets, so that you encourage yourself to live in the real world.

Let us suppose that you have listed all your debts – *all* your debts – and they come to £7000; and all your income, including benefits, and that that comes to £8000. Now the exercise is a profitable one, and all you have to do is set about servicing your debts. It may be an excellent idea to pay off everything while you can. Certainly you will feel a lot better once you have done so, but have you made provision for the unexpected demand that descends upon you like a thunderbolt, before you have had time to put up your umbrella? Try this:

Open a building society account, or a high interest account at your bank. Draw up a list of all your current outgoings from that useful list I gave you in Chapter 1. You find that you have anticipated outgoings of £7000 a year. Divide the sum by 12, making £583.33. Pay that much into the account each month and have the regular payments (gas, electricity, telephone, credit cards, mortgage, whatever) paid out of that account by direct debit or standing order. If you can achieve this, you will be pleasantly surprised to find that you have a little bit over at the end of the year – the sum earned by the interest on the account – and that this may very well do for emergencies. Furthermore you won't have those officious visitors with clipboards knocking at your door.

What if your income is too sporadic to pay a regular monthly sum into the account? If, like me, you are a freelance, you will know very well that it is impossible to anticipate when the money which you have earned will be paid. In this case, take an average of what you have earned during the past three or four years, and if it works out at £12,000 pa, and your regular and predictable out-goings come to £8000 pa, you will need to pay two thirds of what you receive, *when you receive it*, into the high interest account. If you can do that you ought to be able to use the remaining one third for inessentials and having fun (which is not really inessential at all).

But then there is the likelihood that when you have studiously and obediently done your sums as I have suggested, they do not come out so favourably at all. Your regular outgoings come to £7000, your income to £6000. It is at moments such as these that you will have to come to terms with the need to change your life-style.

You may be able to reduce your outgoings, or increase your incomings. I hope that by using the advice contained within this book creatively you will be able to do both. But it is also possible that, no matter how much you work at it, the sums just don't add up. Right then, change your life-style. You own a house? Sell it. You can't, because you're in negative equity? Rent a room. You run a car? Get rid of it. You have no car? Sell something. You've nothing to sell? Take advice.

What is certain is that if you are living beyond your means, and you do not change your life-style but continue to live beyond your means, things can only get worse.

When things get really rough, and you can see no possible way out, you will have to take advice. Try the Citizens Advice Bureau first.

A word or two about these estimable places. They are funded by local councils, with bits and pieces from the National Association and charities. Their aims are twofold: they do their best to ensure that individuals don't suffer from a lack of knowledge as to their rights and responsibilities, and the services available to them; through their first-hand knowledge of the problems faced by those who seek them out they try to influence the development of social policies and services. They emphasise with some passion that they are confidential. Nothing you tell them will be passed on. They are impartial and their services are equally available to everybody 'regardless of race, gender, disability, and to lesbians, gay men, and those living with HIV/AIDS'. They claim to have no preconceived attitudes and they make no charges to their clients. They are committed to equal opportunities to all. Saints.

But I have to report that they were decidedly cagey

with me when I told them that I was researching this book. And did not telephone me back as they had promised.

Each CAB is an independent charity, and employs both paid staff and volunteers. An analysis of the bureaux in the borough I live in showed that in the year ending March 1996, nearly 60,000 cases were dealt with, of which a third related to benefits, and an equal number to 'consumer issues', i.e. employment, housing, legal advice and 'other'. A small but significant percentage dealt with 'relationships', 'taxes', and 'utilities', whatever that may mean.

As I waited for the interview which I was not to be granted I shared the office with an elderly man, who, hearing the title of the book I was writing – this book – muttered: 'You can't.' He was trying to live on £70 a week, having been used to an income of £400. 'I spend out more than I get in – can't help it.' I hoped that the CAB would be able to identify some benefits he should have been receiving and wasn't. So did he.

An additional paragraph at the end of this necessarily painful chapter is called for. Let us assume that you have managed to get relatively straight and decide that you want to remain so. There are significant advantages in the use of Direct Debits. Some companies, notably utility and telephone companies, give a discount of 3–4%, which could come to a welcome £12 a year saved. There is the disadvantage that they may vary the rate without telling you, so you will need to check the bill, even though you may think that you don't have to. And it is no use to ask them to take the money out of your account on such and such a date, because it would fall directly after the

day on which you get your salary cheque. If you want
to choose the date on which you pay you can do so by
a standing order. The disadvantage of this, however, is
that you will not qualify for the discounts, and you will
have to vary the amount of the standing order every time
they tell you that their charges are changing.

But either direct debits or standing orders should help
you to find what is worth more than a small per annum
discount; I mean, peace of mind.

4. Shark-infested Waters

I can't see where the problem lies. Managing one's personal finances is a simple matter. At the beginning of the year I make a liberal estimate of what I am likely to spend. I then assess, conservatively, what I am likely to earn. Then I borrow the difference.

Dr Erich Loening

How things have changed! When I was a student and old enough to be expected to look after my own affairs, I opened a bank account with Barclays, and was handed my first cheque book. I still have the counterfoils; and £2.10s (£2.50) would be enough to look after my weekly requirements. The bank staff would recognise me and greet me cheerily with: 'Good morning, Mr Benedictus!', much in the manner that AA patrolmen would salute the passing cars of AA members identified by one of those classy badges displayed up front.

You only needed a cheque book then. If you had one, you were identified by tradespeople as a person of substance, and your credit was automatically 'good'. How different today when a cheque book without a guarantee card categorises you as, at best, wayward and, at worst, a thief.

Today people are expected, persuaded, and almost required to live by credit. This trend was given momentum

by the Thatcherite 'right to buy' policy. What this meant was that council tenants were encouraged to buy their own homes, and it was made easy for them to do so. The middle-class dream of owning a home turned to a nightmare for many when the council houses they had purchased turned out to be seriously sub-standard, difficult to mortgage, and, as near as dammit, impossible to sell.

Simultaneously with this Thatcherite dream of the eighties, and in part because of it, came the housing boom. Now that it was officially sanctioned that everyone was entitled to own their own home, mortgages at twice, three times your annual salary, were obtainable on the basis of a nod and a wink. House prices soared. And the faster the band-wagon rolled the more desperate the efforts to leap on of those terrified of being left behind.

People who owned a portfolio of blue-chip shares earning them a solid 2.75%, stared in astonishment as it was announced that in the last six months house prices had risen by a further 10%, 20%. It could not last. It did not last. And when the smoke cleared, and prices stablised and then fell, many of the new home-owners, and not a few of the old ones, who had over-extended themselves, found themselves staring at a new and horribly grinning monster called Negative Equity.

The years passed. House prices drifted aimlessly. Repossessions rose as those who could not keep up the mortgage saw their houses sold for a fraction of what they knew them to be worth. Nothing could be depended upon. The manufacturing industries laid off staff, and when new people were brought in, they had short-term contracts at best, and sometimes just piece-work. The black economy flourished. So did the grey.

You thought your pension was assured? Not if it was with Mirror Group Newspapers. You were ever so proud to be invited to become a Lloyds Name? The honour turned out to be a licence to lose everything.

As the old certainties were eroded, credit replaced cash. It was phenomenal how much was available to you if your references were good, and even if they weren't, it was surprising how easy it became to borrow large sums to service smaller ones. And still is.

The tabloid press is filled with advertisements inviting you a) to enjoy telephone sex with Luscious Lucia and b) to borrow, borrow, borrow. The pleasures of both

a) and b) are equally short lived. An IVA (Individual Voluntary Arrangement) which is probably what the ad is all about is a draconian means of offering you large sums of money at naughty interest rates. More about these in Chapter 11.

There are two basic ways of borrowing money. One is secured and one is unsecured. A secured loan is one which gives the person who lends the money the right to seize whatever it is which secures the loan (a house, a car, a business) should the person who borrows the money fail to keep up the payments. This is fun for the lender since they can hardly lose. It is cheaper for the borrower than an unsecured loan. An example of a secured loan is a mortgage, or a bank overdraft with a portfolio of shares as collateral.

An unsecured loan is just about everything else. Credit cards, HP, money from loan sharks, what have you. Shortly after the present government came to power, the Minister for Consumer Affairs announced that high-charging mortgage lenders and home credit companies were under review. Home credit companies (1200 are listed but there are probably many more) are those altruistic folk who come round door-to-door and make small loans to the terminally harassed. Although I obviously cannot list the companies here, it was noticeable that after the Minister's announcement, shares in Provident Financial, Cattles, S & U, and London Scottish Bank, fell sharply. It was pointed out that these home credit companies traditionally charge APRs (annual percentage rates) of between 100% and 500%.

Door-to-door lending has been growing apace in recent years, and the reason seems to be that if you are poor in the UK, you are less likely to have household insurance, life insurance, credit cards or access to other forms of credit. You are also burgled more often, you are subject to cash-flow problems, and you die younger than if you are rich. Sorry.

The problem with being poor (one of many) is that nobody, except the door-to-door lenders, sometimes known as tallymen, is interested in lending money to you because the sums are too small to be of consequence. Local branches of banks have closed; building societies have merged. Where do you go to borrow the pittance that you need at a fair rate? It would be helpful if supermarkets and post offices were to offer subsidised loans based on social security payments. J. Sainsbury's, which has been losing out to Tesco's in the supermarket stakes, has recently initiated its own banking services, Tesco's is to follow suit and Richard Branson has announced the setting up of a banking operation which incorporates your mortgage within your everyday spending patterns.

The Sainsbury's Bank looks promising. You can open an account with as little as £1, enjoy instant access and round-the-clock telephone banking (that is to say you can ring up at two in the morning and find out how much you have in your account before going out and filling up with petrol on your credit card), and receive 1000 reward points (worth £10, although it sounds much more) if you can show that an error has been made on your account. Their rates of interest on both accounts and loans are very fair.

The Branson One Bank initiative will permit borrowing within the limits set down to accommodate your mortgage and any other needs you may have. But it could turn out to be more expensive than the traditional methods of borrowing money. Early days yet.

THE BANK MANAGER'S STORY

I went for a chat with my bank manager.

He said the ideal bank loan is to a chap with an income of £25,000 a year who wants to borrow £5000. The loan should be self-liquidating, that is to say that during the first year the chap will spend £30,000; during the second £20,000, after which bob's your uncle.

Most bank branch managers have discretion for loans up to £15,000. Since all acounts are now computerised, as soon as you reach the limit of your overdraft alarm bells will ring, and all transactions will be scrutinised daily.

'It's not as easy as it used to be,' said the bank manager wryly. 'There was a time when someone in my position would have had 1000 customers to deal with; now I have 3000. I try not to bounce the cheques of my customers, and especially not if I know them personally. Flexibility and personal contact is what the bank can offer, and it's not something you get from First Direct.'

I wondered whether it might not sometimes be deliberate policy to encourage customers to spend up to and beyond the limit of their overdraft, because after all the bank charges a hefty £25 (sometimes more) for each returned cheque, and since a cheque may be automatically presented three times, the unfortunate customer may find himself or herself paying £75 to have a cheque returned, and then having also to pay for the letters which describe the disastrous turn events have taken. Clearly this is not a sensible way to proceed. A returned cheque for £10 can cost the issuer £100 before dying its sad and inconsequential death.

'Tell us early and tell us everything,' implored the bank manager. 'If you don't we will find out anyway. If you tell me that you want an additional overdraft for a home extension and then go and spend it on delinquent debts which you haven't mentioned, how do you imagine we won't know, and what do you imagine that will do to your credit rating next time you want an overdraft?'

The bank manager grew quite sad as he mused over the folly of those he has to deal with. If only they would regard credit cards as a means of payment of bills rather than as a source of additional sums. The rates of interest on even the cheapest card (which are the cheapest cards? See Chapter 5) are exorbitant.

But then so they can be on bank loans. Let us suppose you want to borrow £50 from a bank over a year. It will cost you £96, but if you work out all the figures, including typical bank charges, you will be paying an interest rate of over 600%, and an APR of not much less. Compare that with the rich borrower who requires £10,000 for a year. His/her equivalent rates are 19.9% and an APR of 28%.

I asked my bank manager for a true story with a happy end. He brightened considerably.

'I had this customer who had been unemployed for eighteen months. His wife, who worked part-time, earned a small salary. They had a fairly substantial mortgage, they owed money to the bank, to three credit card companies, and they had taken out several personal loans on the basis of past earnings. They also had mortgage arrears. Nonetheless they had been using their credit cards to pay for their customary life-style, somehow managing to find the minimum payment required on each card each month. Things had got so bad that I was faced with returning their cheques on a daily basis.

'After they came in to see me, I had the overdraft restructured for them, and also worked with them on restructuring their other loans. However, their debts were such that their outgoings were more than their incomings. I insisted that they cut up their credit cards and watched them do it. I offered on their behalf 2.5% of the outstanding debt monthly to each credit card company. I took their cheque books and guarantee cards away. I had an amount transferred to a deposit account for day-to-day expenses.

'That was eighteen months ago. They came to see me two weeks ago. He had found work. They had paid off two of the credit card accounts completely. Their rating had improved considerably as a result of no further cheques being returned. The reason no further cheques had been returned was that neither of them had a cheque book. We arranged to remortgage their property to pay off their outstanding debts, and now they are paying off the residual funds. They are, I have estimated, £350 a month better off. If they had not come to me in the first place, everything would have been bounced. Hopeless.'

In serious cases which don't have happy endings, what the bank manager will do is suspend all interest and charges on the debt, freeze the account including all standing orders and cheque book payments, and discuss with the customer some way of repaying at a later date, when things are looking healthier. The other options are repossessions, voluntary liquidations, and bankruptcy, which I shall be dealing with in a later chapter.

THE MONEY LENDER'S STORY

He didn't look like a shark, and I don't suppose he was. It was a family business, and its offices were in a handsome Gothic building in a classy and expensive town. Certainly he was licensed to lend money, which is a legal requirement, although not one which all money-lenders adhere to. He said that when his clients fall behind with their repayments he suggests renegotiating the loan over a longer period. In extremis he does of course use the courts, but has never resorted to strong arm tactics. If things get heavy it leads to a lot

of aggravation he told me, and that costs money. He said that in America money-lenders cover themselves with high insurance against their clients' inability to pay as a result of unemployment; personally he prefers to rely on his instincts. He will occasionally lend money to self-employed people, he said, it's very much a matter of their past history. Inevitably he checks people's credit references on one (or more) of the freely available data bases.

I wondered what sort of frauds were practised against him. He gave me a typical example. There are people living in other people's houses (or breaking into them, I suppose), who, for the purposes of taking out a loan, get hold of other people's papers – bank statements, salary statements, itemised valuations. With these and an assumed name it is not hard to negotiate credit, without the slightest intention of paying any of it back.

If you ever get a chance to look at a training document for money lenders, you will be surprised and alarmed. I did and I was. These are some of the things the trainees are told.

Personal Unsecured Loans

Personal Unsecured Loans will only be granted to clients in full-time employment and to those who have been in their present jobs for three months at the very least. They will not under any circumstances be granted to married women, or to applicants who have had more than two jobs in the last two years, or to applicants under twenty-one, while those between twenty-one and twenty-five who apply for a loan will be asked to provide a guarantor to co-sign the form with the applicant. So far as married women are concerned, applications must be made in the husband's name, and you will not be surprised to learn that married woman, as well as self-employed people, are not regarded as suitable guarantors.

The trainees are then advised that if they receive an application from someone who does not qualify under the conditions above but who is a house-owner, they should be pressurised to take out a 'POA' and shown an F2 asap. What is a POA? A Property Owner's Advance, of course, and something therefore to make even the most hard-headed loan shark salivate. What is an F2? A form. What is asap? I'll tell you as soon as possible.

So then, having ensured that their client qualifies for an unsecured loan the trainee is encouraged to inquire what you, the borrower, want the money for.

The most acceptable answer is home improvements, which enhance the value of your property. The sensible policy of allowing tax relief on home improvements was revoked a few years ago. Next best are the sort of reasons which anyone would support: my daughter's getting married, my son wants to spend some time in France to help him with his French A-level, and so on. A mysterious addendum to the document which I have in front of me specifies that while the money may acceptably be used for musical instruments, these should not be electronic!

Any other reasons which may be given should not stand in the way of the granting of the loan, but ought to be referred upwards. The lender is not concerned with how the money is to be used so much as how it will be paid back. But it gives both lender and client something jolly to talk about while each assesses the trustworthiness of the other.

The salesman or woman then embarks upon a rigma-role, setting out the terms of the loan and how much the client will be expected to pay per week. The loan will include a life, accident and sickness insurance policy, the cost of which is deducted from the loan upon signature. And it is this insurance policy which provides the sales-man with his or her commission. It is probably worth repeating this in capital letters: NO INSURANCE, NO COMMISSION; and also emphasising that banks, credit card operators, and just about everybody in the world with money to lend will try to include an element of life insurance when they lend you money.

Here is another irony. Not only do your debts die with you, but if you have borrowed money extensively while you are alive, dying could be your best possible career move.

Let us suppose you have been given the figures for the cost of your loan, and you are dithering. You want it, you need it, you love the idea of walking out of this office with a substantial cheque in your sweaty hand, but the implications of the amount of your indebtedness are worrying you. What happens then? The trainee will hit you with the following arguments: if you settle the balance early, you will only be charged interest on the period during which you have had the loan; you can renegotiate the loan later on, reducing it or – more likely – increasing it. Lenders love repeat business; no fees are charged for arranging the loan (this of course is unlike a bank loan when there is usually a fee of £50 or so for setting up an overdraft arrangement); repayments are quoted over the maximum repayment period. If you are able to settle earlier, you will gain peace of mind, but lose out on interest. What a marvellous deal the insurance element is! Probably less than 50p per week, and it means you can die happy.

In the light of these powerful arguments only the most level-headed of clients will be able to resist that vital signature.

The salesman may or may not draw to your attention your statutory right to return the loan and the form within two weeks if you decide you do not want it after all.

If you only require a very small loan, you will be encouraged to consider a larger one. But the cost of a small loan will probably be about £13 per month for £100, with a commission of £2. The APR on that is, of course, disreputably high.

Property Owners Advances (POAs)

The benefit to the lender of such a deal is evident. The loan is secured. As to how they secure the property, that is their affair; all you need to know is that the property you have offered as collateral for this loan will inevitably be at risk if the loan is not repaid in full.

The benefits to you they will spell out in fulsome phrases with many adjectives and probably a bone china cup of coffee if not a glass of sweet sherry.

Repayments may be spread over anything from three to fifteen years, and the longer the period the lower the monthly outgoings you will be expected to have to pay. Comparisons will be made with the excessive rates charged by short-term loans, credit card companies, and

HP deals. It will be emphasised that there need be no interference with existing mortgage arrangements, that complete confidentiality will be assured, that loans may be settled early without penalty, that how you use the money is no concern of theirs, that the self-employed are welcomed, and so too are clients with court orders, mortgage arrears, and other beastly things hanging around their necks.

All of which, of course, is undeniable. The only questions you need to ask are: What am I getting myself into? What is it going to cost me? Can I do better elsewhere? Am I ever realistically going to be able to pay them back? What happens if I can't?

Hire Purchase

'Buying on the HP' is how we used to live in the days when televisions had little doors in front of the screen, and men wore flat hats at football matches. Credit cards and bank loans have replaced the HP agreement (or Conditional Sale as it is more accurately known) for most purchases, but major items, and especially cars, are still frequently bought in this way.

What it means, of course, is that you don't own the car until you have paid the full amount owed. But in the minefield known as credit, things are never that simple.

What you have to bear in mind is:

1. For sales up to £15,000 agreements are regulated under the Consumer Credit Act.
2. Your contract is with the finance company and not with the garage (although some garages run their own finance agreements). This can work in your

favour if the car is not what it purports to be – if you can show that the mileage has been 'clocked' for example – or if it is faulty.

3. You can't sell the car (or whatever the item is) until you've completed the purchase, without the written permission of the creditor.

4. You can surrender the car to the finance company ('the hirer') at any time during your agreement. If you do, and if less than half the total purchase price of the car has been paid, you have to pay the difference between the payments you've already made and half the price of the car, plus any other payments which have become due by the surrender date. If you've paid more than half the purchase price, all you are liable for is any arrears on your previous HP payments.

5. If you've paid more than one third of the total cost, the creditor is not allowed to come round and drive your car away without a court order to that effect.

6. Even if you haven't paid a third, the creditor is only allowed to take your car away if it is on 'public ground'. The law is a bit vague here, but it seems that the hirer can't repossess the car if it's in your garage or your drive.

7. If you want to keep the car, but have fallen behind with your payments, you should still be able to. In this case you will have received a Default Notice, a Calling in Notice or a Termination Notice. Now it gets complicated. You must go to the *County Court* and ask for a Time Order, on a form known as an N440. This will cost you £50, I'm afraid, unless you're on Income Support, in which case it's free. If you're not on Income Support, but your income is low, you

can ask the court to waive their fee. But for this you'll need an Application for a Fee Remission form.

If the creditor has already been to court for a Return of Goods Order and you've received a summons, you can ask for your Time Order without paying a fee (aha!). In which case you have to ask the *County Court Office* for an N244.

Then you can request that the Return of Goods Order is suspended on condition that you pay a fixed amount per month. If you keep up to date with these repayments, your creditor won't be able to get a *County Court* judgement against you (and would be stupid to try because it would cost a fair amount of money).

An example may help:

	£
The total price of your car, including the HP, was	10,000.00
You've already paid	3000.00
Difference between half the price of the car and what you've paid is	2000.00
But you've fallen behind with your payments by	500.00
And you ran into a lamp-post and to repair the wing will cost you a further	250.00
Therefore, if you decide to surrender the car, you must pay	2750.00

But if the finance company ends the agreement, the sums look like this:

	£
The total price of the car, including the HP, was	10,000.00
But you've only paid	3000.00
And your arrears are	500.00
And they sell the car for a further	5000.00
Therefore, they are within their rights to demand from you	2500.00

Whatever you do, don't try and sell the car privately without having their consent in writing, because you will be Breaking the Law.

Once you've done your sums – bearing in mind that the finance company may sell the car to the garage you originally bought it from at a knock down price – you can make an informed decision as to whether or not to surrender the car. If you do, you will at least avoid a good deal of hassle.

By the way, if you live in Scotland, the procedures are different. Once you have received a Notice, you need to go to the Sheriff Court for a Time To Pay Direction. Fuller details at the end of Chapter 10.

5.   The Nitty Gritty

The difference between a dead skunk and a dead banker on the road is that there are skid marks by the skunk.

Anon

What follows is, I hope, some solid advice on the most attractive offers in the borrowing market. But first of all an explanation of that mysterious mantra, known as APR.

APR stands for Annual Percentage Rate, and is a worthy attempt to find a way of comparing different rates charged by different lenders. When you add all charges, agent's and surveyor's fees, and other associated costs, to the basic interest, and distribute the total costs across the period of the loan, then, expressed as an annual rate, you end up with the APR.

But bear in mind that even comparing APR rates can be misleading, because they don't take into account *how* people charge interest. Some credit card companies, for instance, charge interest on purchases from the date of purchase of the goods (bad), while others, such as Cyprus Popular, only charge interest from the date of the statement (good). Sometimes, too, there will be no interest-free repayment period if money is still owing from a previous statement.

Nonetheless I shall have to stick with APR, until somebody comes up with something better.

It is also important to understand the difference between the different kinds of plastic.

Credit Cards. Most credit card companies offer you an interest-free loan from the date of purchase. If you repay monthly in full there is no reason why you should be charged any interest – the company receives a royalty from the shop at which you use your card, so they're all right – and if you don't repay in full, you will be required to pay back a minimum of between 3% and 5% of the balance each month.

Visa and Access are examples. With many of these cards you get one useful concession: extra protection if the retailer from whom you have ordered your goods goes bust, or if the goods which you have bought on your card are faulty.

Some credit cards require an annual fee, usually between £8 and £20, and APRs charged by credit card companies vary from 11% to 30%, so you can clearly see why it is necessary to shop around before committing yourself to the one with the most persuasive come-on advertising.

Almost all cards (with the exception of Amex) are linked to the Mastercard or Visa systems, making them valid overseas, and acceptable to cash dispensers.

There is an art to the use of credit cards. If you make your purchases on the day on which your statement is due, you have a calendar month before that purchase appears on your bill, and a further 26 days, or thereabouts, to pay without penalty. When you think about it, that adds up to almost two months of interest-free credit.

Which magazine (August 1997) reported that the best cards without an annual fee are the People's Bank of Connecticut, Mastercard/Visa, Bank of Cyprus, and MBNA (which allows up to 57 days of free credit). The best cards which impose an annual fee are Bank of Scotland, Barclaycard, Lloyds, Midland, Natwest, and the Royal Bank of Scotland.

These are the most competitive monthly interest rates currently being charged:

	%
TSB up to	1.67
Lloyds up to	1.62
Barclaycard	1.61
NatWest	1.56
Midland	1.55

Easily the cheapest, however, is the People's Bank, Connecticut at just 1.13% with no annual fee and an interest-free period.

It is worth noting that percentage rates are often shown per calendar month because they are far less frightening in this form.

Many of the cards offer interesting perks, which may even be in the form of charitable donations, but are usually travel accident insurance cover, points schemes, defective goods insurance, and the offer of an emergency cash card for those embarrassing moments. MBNA has the most meaningful perks (if you pay in full). The Alliance and Leicester has a cash rebate reward for prompt payment. If you occasionally pay in full the recommendation is the Alliance and Leicester Money Back Card. If you never pay in full, then go for the Save & Prosper Base rate Linked Card.

Charge Cards are those which require you to pay back the whole amount of your credit each month. Examples are Amex and Diners Club. There is usually no serious limit on your borrowings, and you pay higher fees only if you fail to pay within fifty-six days of your statement (or, in some cases, purchase). If you are a prompt payer, there is no reason not to use a charge card.

Gold Cards are the same as charge cards, but with more cachet. You are usually only qualified to receive one if you earn at least £20,000 a year. Their annual fees are quite high – at least £35 in most cases – and you may expect the APR to be between 10% and 21%. It used to be the case that the possession of a Gold Card entitled you to almost unlimited credit. This concession has been removed in most cases, although the clients have not always been told that it has. Since there is usually an annual fee attached to the privilege of possessing a Gold Card, such behaviour is really quite naughty.

Store Cards. Increasingly the chains of high street stores and supermarkets are trying to develop customer loyalty. They may do this through 'Club Cards', 'Reward Cards', 'Loyalty Cards' and such like. They are even more anxious to rope you in to their Store Card system, which has two benefits for them: you tend to buy more goods at their store; you tend to use the credit they are offering you rather than the credit which Visa, Access, Mastercard, and Amex are offering you, and upon which the store has, of course, to pay a royalty. Although as an account holder you will probably receive some perks from the store, you should bear in mind that the APR on these store cards is traditionally high, anything up to 33% in fact. You're better off using a cheque on your current account, or cash.

It might be useful at this point to set out the different forms of borrowing available to you, their advantages and disadvantages, and a few recommendations.

Bank Overdrafts

Good: Unless you have to pay fees, these may be a cheap form of borrowing, particularly if you stay within your limit. Fees are usually about £8 a month.

Bad: If you have an unauthorised over-spend they can become expensive (30% in the case of *Clydesdale* and *NatWest*). Also, and disgracefully, some banks charge £15 and upwards to send you a letter to tell you you're overdrawn without permission. Bounced cheques, standing orders, and direct debits are usually charged at £20 or £25 a time.

The big four English high street banks make a charge for current account overdrafts (although some have recently brought in a small degree of flexibility). At the time of writing the best banks and building societies for personal loans with their APRs are as follows:

For £1000 over one year

	APR
Beneficial Bank	15.9
Chelsea Building Society	15.9
Bank of Scotland Direct	15.8
Yorkshire Building Society	15.0
Sainsbury's Bank	12.7

For £5000 over three years

Chelsea Building Society	13.8
Yorkshire Building Society	13.8
Beneficial	13.7
Alliance and Leicester	13.3
Hamilton Direct Bank	12.9
Sainsbury's Bank	12.8

For £10,000 over five years

Automobile Association	12.7
Alliance and Leicester	12.7
Sainsbury's Bank	12.7
Yorkshire Building Society	12.7
Bank of Scotland Direct	12.6
Bank of Scotland	12.5
Hamilton Direct Bank	12.5

If you need a loan with instant access, then the best currently on offer are, for sums under £1000, the Clydesdale Bank and Sainsbury's Bank. For sums over £1000, the best are Cheltenham and Gloucester, Clydesdale and Scottish Widows.

Secured Loans

Good: A loan secured on your house, investments, or other collateral, is cheaper than an unsecured loan, and easier to arrange.

Bad: There may be additional costs associated with valuing your property and legal fees. If you fall behind with your repayments you put your house at risk – it could be repossessed.

Unsecured Loans

Good: It may be simple and quick to organise one and is therefore seriously tempting.

Bad: Interest rates are high, and may be extortionate. You may not qualify (see the Money Lender's Story, p.58).

Insurance Policy Loans

This is a loan taken out against an endowment policy.

Good: The interest is low and there is flexibility on the repayments.

Bad: You need to have a suitable policy already in order to qualify.

In conclusion there is a praiseworthy initiative imported from the USA, which deserves more exposure than it receives. I refer to the Credit Unions. The idea is simple and time-honoured: a savings and loans co-operative run by its members on behalf of its members, not dissimilar, I suppose, to the original building and friendly societies. The committee which considers each loan application on its merits is enabled to lend monthly as much as the Union has received in savings from its better-off members. In the USA the movement has over 30 million members and its operations account for about 15% of consumer credit.

By June 1997 there were 394 Credit Unions in the United Kingdom, the largest concentration being in the North West (114) and Scotland (113). In 1995, the latest year for which we have complete figures, loans amounting to just over £74 million were made. For full details of the movement and how to set one up if you feel the spirit move you contact: The Association of British Credit Unions, Holyoake House, Hanover Street, Manchester, M60 0AS. Tel: 0161 832 3694. Fax: 0161 832 3706.

But whatever you borrow, how much, from whom, and in whatever circumstances, you must ensure that you are healthily suspicious, that you read all the small print, that you are not leaping into something you really cannot afford merely because you can see an alleviation of your short-term problems, and that, if possible, you take advice from someone who can look at your circumstances objectively. I wish I could remember the shaggy dog story about the father giving his son advice about strangers in pubs. It ends something like this: 'So, son, if a stranger approaches you and bets you £100 that he has a dog which can squirt cider straight into your left ear, don't touch it, son, 'cos, sure as hell, you're going to end up with an ear full of cider.'

6.   Selling the Family Silver

I'll tell thee everything I can:
There's little to relate.
I saw an aged, aged man,
A-sitting on a gate.

'Who are you, aged man?' I said.
'And how is it you live?'
And his answer trickled through my head
Like water through a sieve.

He said, 'I look for butterflies
That sleep among the wheat:
I make them into mutton-pies,
And sell them in the street.'

from *Alice Through the Looking-Glass* by
Lewis Carroll (chap. 7)

Times were hard. Among the bits and pieces floating
about the house, and costing several quid in insurance,
was a diamond ring I had inherited. The valuation for
insurance purposes at the time of the inheritance was
£6200. It was a pretty ring, with a pair of diamonds on
a white gold shank, and my circumstances were such
that the odd £6000 would improve them considerably.
But how to set about selling it?

My first port of call was the local jewellers who had

done the original valuation some six or seven years before. I took in the ring and the valuation. They looked dubious. I saw glances being exchanged between the sales staff.

'But you're lucky,' they said.

'I'm glad to hear it.'

'Very lucky indeed. Because today's the day.'

'Tremendous.'

'Today's the day on which the gentleman calls.'

'I *am* lucky. Why does he call?'

'He calls to take away items which have been brought in for valuation.'

'Why does he do that?'

'To value them.'

'But of course.'

'And when does he bring them back?'

'Monday. And when he tells us what your ring is actually worth, we'll be able to make you an offer.'

'Dandy. But isn't it – or rather a few years ago wasn't it? – worth £6200?'

I saw the looks passing across the shop-floor again, and I could interpret them. 'We've got a right one here,' was what they were clearly saying, and implying that I was another innocent who had not understood the difference between valuation *for probate* and valuation *for insurance*.

When someone dies the beneficiaries of the will don't want to pay death duties if they can help it – currently the first £300,000 of an inheritance is free of duties, so in most cases you won't have to pay anyway – and a friendly valuation for probate will ensure that any indebtedness to the Chancellor is kept to the minimum. Valuation for insurance puts a high figure on an item because while it will not make much difference to the premiums you have to pay, it will make a big difference to the replacement value if the item is lost or stolen. Valuers like high valuations because it suggests that you may return to them for the replacement, and if you do so you will have pots to spend.

Doesn't the difference between the two valuations smack of dishonesty? Yes. Doesn't the government lose out in death duties as a result if this practice is widespread? Yes. How would people feel if I were to produce two sets of accounts, one showing a massive profit on my trading to impress those whom I need to impress, the other showing that I was barely breaking even, in order to avoid paying tax? They would be shocked.

I returned to the jewellers, as instructed, the following Monday.

'Nice ring.'

'Isn't it though?'

'Problem is, we're not interested in buying right now.'

'*Anything*?'

'That ring.'

'And its valuation? I appreciate that it might not be easy to sell it at £6200, the value you put on it six years ago for insurance purposes, but all the same . . .'

'We wouldn't care to give you a figure.'

'None at all?'

'No.'

I decided to visit a West End auctioneer, and discovered that next to the entrance to the sale rooms was a jolly little shop full of diamond rings and other bits and bobs. The woman in the shop looked at the ring and asked: 'How much are you hoping to get?' (From my time in the business of buying and selling I have learned that this is the standard question asked by anyone who sniffs a potential bargain. Despite the popularity over many years of the Antiques Road Show, there are still people who don't realise that they may be sitting on a very desirable item. So innocent are some of them that they name a figure so far below the market value that the buyer cannot resist snapping up a bargain. It's an easy question to ask; a hard one to answer.)

When I refused to be drawn on specifics, she came up with a very fair offer. 'See what the auctioneer suggests as an estimate for your ring, and I will match the upper figure. In cash. And you won't have to wait for your money. And you won't have to pay commission.'

The auctioneer's jewellery valuer was a charming, bustling sort of woman with the reassuring good looks of Delia Smith, and the heart-warming accents of Jenni Murray. She took the ring and the valuation away, and returned with both, and a less than reassuring expression. First she softened me up by telling me that the diamonds were mining diamonds – I supposed that all diamonds were – and that that was good, and that they were probably Victorian and that that was all right. They were not, however, a pair, one being square-cut and one not.

'Your valuer claims that the ring is 1.25 carats. We don't believe it is. For a diamond the carat is a magic sign. More than a carat is good; less than a carat, not so hot. We don't know why they gave the weight as 1.25. The only way to be sure would be to remove the stones from the setting and weigh them. Do you want us to do this?'

'Not really. What I hoped for was a written estimate.'

Early Renoir - two a penny - we get them all the time

'If we entered it in our next jewellery sale we would put down an estimate of £600–£800.'

I did not return to the little shop next to the auctioneers. I went home gloomily on the crowded tube, thinking how quickly £6200 can become £600–£800.

Not far from the jewellers who had originally valued the ring is a more modest establishment with an A-board outside. 'Good money paid for gold, silver, diamonds, jewellery', it proclaimed. What other kind of money is there, I wondered sourly, but, being in a what-the-hell mood, I went in.

'You're lucky,' they told me. Everyone kept telling me that. 'This is the valuer's afternoon in. He was about to leave.'

The valuer emerged from a back-room, and shook my

hand. 'My name's Dave,' he said, 'what's yours?' I told him, and we chuckled at the coincidence. 'What have you got to sell me then?' said Dave. I showed him the ring and the by now rather crumpled valuation. He grunted. 'I won't waste your time,' he said. 'I work in Hatton Garden most of the week, and this is the sort of ring I can sell. How much were you hoping to get for it?'

'I realise that the valuation is a bit optimistic,' I said, 'But all the same . . .' I thought fast. 'Not a penny less than £2000.'

'OK,' said Dave, 'I don't mess around. It's a deal.'

'How much?'

'What you said. £2000.'

The speed with which he had accepted my figure alarmed me. I was also bewildered. How could it be that an auctioneer would be willing to put a top estimate of £800 on a ring, for which a Hatton Garden dealer called Dave would pay £2000 in readies?

'No questions asked,' Dave added.

'I said not a penny less than £2000,' I said, to Dave's evident disapproval, 'I didn't say £2000.'

Dave did not waste time. He gave me his Hatton Garden card. 'I shall be there on Monday. The offer's open until then. Otherwise forget it.' It was Friday. I had the week-end in which to make up my mind. But I still had one other resource.

Old friends of the family run a highly-respected jeweller's shop. I thought the time had come to ask advice from experts, and these were experts, if expert means anything at all. I hoped my experiences might amuse them. They invited me to lunch on the Monday. Every lunchtime the family have a director's lunch in a room underneath the shop; it is a substantial meal with the best roast potatoes I have ever tasted, and no stinting. They were amused by my adventures, but at the same time they were professional. Between courses they took my ring away, polished it up a bit, and examined it. Their first words were not altogether encouraging.

'You must not necessarily assume that any offer is a bad offer,' they told me. '£2000 seems pretty fair. You could do a lot worse.'

The paterfamilias, who had not examined the ring, but had enjoyed the discussion, gave his view.

'Give David £2050,' he said. 'After all he's had a lot of travelling, and I've found his story very interesting. Would you like cash?'

There are questions which arise and conclusions which may be drawn from my experiences selling the ring. Assuming that you are not fortunate enough to have such enlightened friends, how do you make sure that you won't be ripped off by a shady operator, and part with a priceless heirloom for a pittance? Clearly you must have several opinions. An antiques fair can be useful if what you have to sell is antique. Ask a number of the stall-holders to give you their very best price and tell them frankly that you will be prepared to sell to whomsoever makes the highest offer. Once you have a useful guide-line from several sources you can then answer the question: 'How much were you hoping to get?' with 'Not a penny less than X.' This technique will certainly work if what you have is clearly of value; a largish piece of silver or gold plate, for example. (If what you have is silver or gold, many of the top dealers may be found clustered in the Hatton Garden area of London.)

I would not entirely discourage you from using auctions, although I have been more frequently disappointed than delighted by selling things in the sale-room. There are also the following disadvantages: you may have to wait a while for your money; there may not be a suitable sale for several months, and most auctioneers have a regrettable policy of not settling up for a month at least after the sale; they may charge you for insurance while they hold the item before the sale, for the cost of photographing it for the catalogue, and – of course – commission, plus VAT on the commission. I was once asked by the friend of an old gentleman who had had to leave his house to sell some small disposable items on his behalf. I took them to an auction house. The total proceeds of the sale of his items was £278. After numerous deductions he received a cheque for just £80.

If you have a rough idea of the value of the items to be auctioned you may, of course, put a reserve on them, thus ensuring that they won't be sold for a derisory sum, but if they fail to reach their reserve you will be faced with a 'buying-in charge' – normally some 2.5% of the reserve. If you have time enough you could traipse around the major houses, Sotheby's, Christie's, Bonham's and Phillips, all of which have branches throughout the UK, asking each of them for their terms of trade and an estimate, and selecting the best. For goods of real value the usual commission rate of 10% plus 10% buyers' premium may be negotiable.

Other options are available to you. One is to advertise your goods in the pages of *Exchange and Mart* or *Loot*, or your local newspaper. *Exchange and Mart* and *Loot* insert your *for sale* ads free, although they make a modest charge for their renewal service – £5 for three consecutive issues, £7 for five, £10 for ten in the case of *Loot*. You may choose to include the price you hope to receive, adding 'no offers' if you are not prepared to bargain, or ONO or OVNO (meaning 'or near offer', 'or very near offer') if you are. You may choose not to include your home telephone number, in which case you should use one of the private box numbers which the magazines offer advertisers.

There are several specialist magazines, which will give you an idea of the sort of prices specialist items may fetch, and in which you may advertise your own. This has the great advantage of directly reaching collectors who may be interested in what you have to sell. I was so inundated with offers for an old Bernard Darwin golfing book, seriously underpriced at £10, after I put an advertisement in *Book and Magazine Collector* (a fascinating publication, available monthly in all large branches of W.H. Smith's and John Menzies), that dealing with huge numbers of disappointed golfing enthusiasts and dealers in golfiana stretched my tact to the limit.

If you wish to know which publications take classified advertisements in specialist areas of collection, trot along to the largest local branch of Smith's or Menzies and have a look.

Most public libraries include on their shelves Antique Price Guides, such as those published by Miller's. These illustrate a range of antiques, chandeliers, as it might be, or toy soldiers, or wine glasses, with the prices they achieved at public auction in the year leading up to publication. The bigger public libraries will also stock specialist price guides, devoted to such things as militaria, jewellery, dolls, or even modest biscuit tins.

If you do have some decent things then you might consider attending an antiques fair. There are specialist fairs too, for things like books, stamps and postcards, records, cassettes and CDs, art deco, and suchlike. To take a stand at an antiques fair will cost you about £25 for the day – considerably more if it's an especially smart fair – and you will be dealing with hard-headed dealers and collectors, who will most likely know more about the value of your goods than you do. Beware! This is not a situation to be encouraged. Nonetheless at an antiques fair you may need to sell just a single item to cover your costs for the day, and, if you feel confident about your pricing it is not necessarily an option to be ignored.

It is more likely that you have no treasures or heirlooms of any significant value, just a good deal of clutter. This can still be turned into cash at a car boot sale. To give some idea of the popularity of the car boot sale in the nineties, it is confidently estimated that many more people attend a car boot sale on a Sunday morning than go to church. Currently the cost of taking your car into one of these intriguing places is about £7, and you can find details of them through the leisure and classified columns of your local paper. It is not a bad idea to turn up at a car boot sale the week before the one at which you are thinking of selling, and checking it out. Are there empty spaces? If not, you will need to turn up a good deal earlier than the official opening time in order to get a decent pitch. Car boots are strictly first come, first serve.

Having decided to give it a go, you must be careful that you will not be out of pocket as a result. If you pay £7 for your pitch and take £6, you will feel aggrieved at having wasted a perfectly good Sunday morning, and coughed up a pound for the privilege of doing so. I usually expect to sell anything between 5% and 10% of the total value of my stock at a car boot sale, so if your stock is valued at £50, forget it.

Ideally you will need a car with a boot, or an estate car, the greater the capacity the better, a fold-up or trestle table, a table cloth, a good book for when things are quiet, a thermos of hot tea or coffee for when things are cold (car boot sales at 7 a.m. can be dreadfully cold), a float made up of a variety of small denomination coins, pens and sticky labels. You don't even need to have a table. Laying things out on a rug, as though in a middle-eastern souk, is perfectly acceptable.

When it comes to knowing how to price your goods, my advice would be to start by pricing things high, reducing them as the morning wears on. Everyone will try to knock down your prices anyway. It's often a good plan to have a rubbish section where everything is priced at £1 or 50p; that, after all, is how Marks and Spencer and Woolworths made their millions.

You may find that the excitement of the occasion and the camaraderie catch your imagination. If you decide to become a regular car boot seller, you will need to know how to replenish your stocks, which falls a little outside the scope of this book. However, I believe it is often possible to make a fair amount of pocket money by buying large job lots at local auctions, and pricing the items individually. You will end up with a colourful, if unclassy, stall; but at least the risk has been spread. Work towards a mark-up of 100%. That is to say if you buy a job lot containing fifty items and reckon that on average you can sell them for £1 apiece, be prepared to pay £25 for the lot. In the old days it was possible to make an excellent living in Brighton, buying in the junk shops of Kemp Town and selling the same items at inflated prices in The Lanes.

You may have a flair for this kind of thing; you may not. It is therefore critically important that you should keep a record of all your outgoings and incomings. The outgoings will not only include the cost of the goods you buy, and the entrance money to be paid to the car boot sale organisers. They must also include the cost of the petrol, wear and tear on your car, the purchase of the stickers you attach to the items, *everything*. More lists, I'm afraid! Let us say that at the end of a month you find that you have incurred expenses of £752.75p and incomings of £830.82, you might feel justifiably pleased with your new enterprise. You might reasonably suppose that you ought to be able to enhance your profits with experience. So you might. But there's one other sum you need to do, and that is to divide the profit you have made by the hours of application to which you have committed yourself. A profit of £78.07p in a month. Not bad, huh? But if that represents forty-one hours of hard slog, you have been working for yourself for less than £2 an hour, which is not to be encouraged. If these are the sort of figures you have come up with, then I suggest there may be a more profitable way to spend such leisure hours as your life-style may provide.

With which in mind, I glanced down the classified pages of the local newspaper, to see what sort of casual work was on offer. I ignored the rather grander display advertisements because most of these were for full-time workers, and called for knowledge, qualifications, skills, or previous experience – sometimes all of the above. The first thing I observed about the small ads was that not too many of them specified what the pay actually amounted to. I do not believe you ought to go along for an interview without first telephoning and asking something about the hours and conditions of work and what one might realistically expect to earn. Just ask, and if the answer is evasive, cross that one off your list. There were calls for book-keepers, canvassers, carpet and upholstery cleaners, plumbers, carpenters, secretaries, market-researchers, 'agents for new products' (sounded a bit suspicious that one), catalogue and leaflet distributors, fence erectors ('even for one-off job'), labourers, bricklayers, forklift truck drivers, stock collectors for a charity shop, cleaners, typists, waiters and kitchen staff, beauty therapists and barbers, dental receptionists and nurses, part-time sales staff and drivers. There was even an advertisement for a part-time audio typist to work in an independent financial advisers. Could be useful, that one.

Curiously the first local newspaper I glanced at had no *Jobs Wanted* section, suggesting that most of those who wish to be accommodated are being accommodated. Conversely if you look in the windows of your newsagents or on the display boards in your branch post office you will find people offering their services in such arcane areas as poodle-trimming, catering, and re-upholstery. For a small weekly charge this may be a sensible way of sharing with the world whatever special skills you may have.

In short there is work out there, and there may even be work advertised which you can do at home – if you have small chidren or disabilities or obligations which make it hard for you to go out to work. Working at home is sufficiently important to deserve its own chapter. It may be a shortish one, but it could cheer things up no end.

7. Home Free

. . . only The Master shall praise us, and only The Master shall blame; And no-one shall work for money, and no-one shall work for fame, But each for the joy of the working, and each, in his separate star, Shall draw the Thing as he sees It for the God of things as They are!

from 'When Earth's Last Picture' by Rudyard Kipling.

These are some of the considerations if you decide to earn extra money from working at home.

Do you have children/ invalids/ dogs/ spouses or partners at home? If you do, what hours do you have to set aside to cater to their requirements, and what is the maximum amount of time you can possibly keep to yourself?

How about space? Do you have a room or a corner of a room, no matter how pokey, which you can devote entirely to your work? You will need space. Do you need storage space, which you don't have? It might be a good idea to turf the car out of the garage (if you have a car and a garage) and use the garage as a work or storage space.

You may find – I hope you do – that your earning potential is such that by working at home you can afford to hire somebody else to undertake some of the domestic chores; walking the dogs, bathing the granny, taking the children to school, shopping, gardening, cleaning, whatever. Or you may find that it makes good financial sense to invest in labour-saving devices which will enable you to complete the chores more speedily. A large fridge-freezer means less frequent shopping, for instance. A dish-washing machine may save you a precious half-hour a day.

It is possible that under the terms of your tenancy, or mortgage, you are not allowed to work at home. If what you intend to do is on a small scale (which at first it probably will be) I suggest you don't worry too much about permissions and small print, but it would be very sensible to have solicitors check the position for you, if things are becoming seriously time and space-consuming. It would be rash to turn your living room into an iron-foundry or a livery stables without a word to a soul. And if things are becoming professional, it may affect the rateable value of your house.

What about insurance? Most householders' policies will not cover you if you are conducting a business from home. This could be serious, because the insurers might refuse to pay out on a claim which arose out of something purely domestic. If you are giving private coaching or doing a bit of mild secretarial work on the side, you may think I am being fussy, but a telephone call to the insurers could be a sensible investment.

Things are not necessarily straightforward. An example: you have skills in repairing china; you took a course in it some years back, and now it seems the ideal way of earning extra money. You advertise locally, and business begins to come your way. That nice management consultant from Number 5 brings you in his precious Worcester vase, because there is a disfiguring crack across the base. You drop it. It shatters into a thousand pieces. That nice management consultant turns nasty. He shows you his valuation for insurance. £3,500. Ouch! You are liable and your insurance won't touch it because it doesn't belong to you. All you would have needed to be covered would have been a codicil to your existing policy, and that is not going to cost an arm and a leg, probably not even a little finger.

And your car . . . is that covered for business purposes? Probably not.

What about the money your new and flourishing business is earning you? The great temptation is to use it to make up the shortfall in the weekly housekeeping, or to pay for those small extras which you have wanted so passionately and so hopelessly for so long. But be very clear. Although you have earned it – and how! – the money does not yet belong to you. It belongs to the business, and may need to be ploughed back into the business, to buy a fax machine, or to repay the bank loan with which you started. Be alert, too, to the additional costs your new enterprise may engender in the household bills. Extra heat and light, that sort of thing. You are using your battered old computer? It will depreciate more quickly now that you are giving it so much more to do. Depreciation is worked out (for tax purposes) by the difference in the cost of buying the thing, and what you may expect to get for it when you sell it, divided by the number of years you are using it.

I hope all this does not discourage you from going into business on your own account. There is good news as well. Many local authorities make 'start-up' grants to those with the initiative to take the plunge. Make an appointment to see yours and ask them.

Now that you have become what they call a sole trader you really ought to open a bank account in the name of the business, and as soon as you really believe the business can afford to do so, start drawing a salary. You do need to keep accounts from the start, and while a neat little cash book will probably do initially, it is advisable to employ an accountant if you feel inadequate to do the detailed work yourself. But beware. An accountant's time can be very expensive, and it is much preferable to teach yourself book-keeping. Many councils run adult evening classes for do-it-yourself accountants.

I am delighted to say that the tax position you will find yourself in once your home-run business begins to flourish, falls well beyond the scope of this book, but the Inland Revenue service publishes a pamphlet called 'Starting in Business' (**IR 28**), which you can obtain from tax offices.

And now that the money is beginning to flow, alarm bells clang. What about that vital Income Support, and the other benefits that have kept you afloat during the lean years? Well, the rules are very clear. If you find yourself working more than sixteen hours a week, or if you have a partner who is working more than twenty-four hours a week, you will lose the right to Income Support or Jobseeker's Allowance, and this could be Very Bad News Indeed. Do you declare your casual labour to the benefits office? Up to you. If you are working more than you ought to be in order to claim benefit, and if you don't declare it, you are breaking the law. This applies, I am afraid to say, whether or not you are working from home.

But back to basics. You are starting out. What will you need?

1. *Business cards.* You can get these printed, decently enough and inexpensively, at the little machines at stations and post offices, and they will probably do for the time being.

2. *Headed notepaper, and printed invoices.* The problem for many, and probably most, small businesses run from home is late payers.

   Figures issued by the Credit Insurance Association show that 31% of businesses fail because of management failure, 20% because of a decline in the cash flow, and 11% because of bad debts. Nearly one in five major companies is guilty of paying late; a practice which is estimated to cost their creditors 2 billion pounds a year. It is deplorable but true that many finance directors get brownie points by delaying payments to small suppliers as long as possible, and telephone receptionists are adept at the white lie that turneth away wrath. How often do you hear: 'I'm ever so sorry; he's in a meeting' or 'I'm afraid you've just missed the monthly cheque run.' The European Commission is shortly to bring forward proposals for a statutory right to interest on debt and the British Government, encouraged by the Forum of Private Business, has promised to adopt a similar policy. But in the meantime if you are one of the sufferers there are two resources which you may find helpful. You can offer a discount on those who pay quickly, say 5% for those who pay within ten working days. Or you can print on your invoices 'Payment within thirty days'. Although this does not have much validity in law, it may make future demands for payment more persuasive, strengthening your hand when you come to chase up those who haven't paid. The law says that you can only enforce any late payment demands if you have agreed terms in writing when you contracted the work. With very late payers, a threat to take them to the small claims court, or a summons, often does the trick. They may be concerned that you will contact their other clients, or the paper(s) in which they had advertised their services. Most people do intend to pay, but delay those payments which seem uncritical until the last possible moment.

In Britain the Small Claims Court is there to help the unfortunate who has suffered from late payments or no payments at all, and although the process of going through a small claims court claim is made as easy as possible there are obvious drawbacks. You can claim up to £3000 – although this is likely to be upped to £5000 soon – but there seems to be no reason why you should not make more than one claim. And if you get a judgement in your favour, it is still up to you to arrange to collect the money, which may well involve bailiffs. It is quite possible that you will be left even more out of pocket as a result.

Professor John Baldwin, of Birmingham University, has spent four depressing years researching into what happened to ninety-four plaintiffs who had won their cases in the small claims courts. Within six months only half of them had received the money which the courts had ordered to be paid to them, while more than a third never received any money at all.

3. *Leaflets to put through doors in your neighbourhood.* If you have a personal computer and a printer you may be quite able to produce your own; the main expense then will be the paper, and the envelopes (if any). The best paper quality comes from art shops, the best selection of stationery at far and away the lowest prices comes from printers not newsagents. A manilla envelope which costs 38p in a small newsagent's shop will cost about 4p if bought in a box of 200 at a printers.

   If you can get your local paper to run an article about your enterprise, that represents priceless publicity, priceless in both senses, because it won't cost you a penny.

4. *A telephone extension and/or an answering machine, a fax and a photocopier* could be wise and tax deductible investments if you intend working in a room without a telephone. If you can run to it it is an excellent idea to have a separate business number; because it does not always sound too professional when a potential client finds himself talking to a four-year-old child. He may be charmed but it is probable that he will take his business elsewhere.

   The great advantage of a business line is that it ought to qualify you for a free entry in Yellow Pages, and you are allowed to choose the category under which you will be listed.

   If your business involves a good deal of phoning, try making as many of those calls as possible during the cheap times. After 6 p.m. is cheapest, which is why you usually get a plethora of double-glazing salesmen cold-calling you as soon as you sit down to supper.

An admirable publication by the Consumers Association, called *Earning Money at Home*, which was published in 1979, and has been revised and reprinted several
times since, gives details of the sort of jobs which those
contemplating working at home should consider, with
much practical information.

Those areas of work, which require previous experience are: beauty therapist, hairdresser, book-keeper, lin-
guist, teacher including music teaching, foreign language
teaching and coaching for exams, typing, word processing, computer training or trouble-shooting (could
I use you!), cooking and catering, drawing and illu-
strating, dressmaking, knitting, photography, printing,
photocopying, repairs including furniture, clothes and
antiques, book binding, bee-keeping, picture-framing,
upholstery, writing – see the invaluable *Writers' and Artists' Yearbook* (A and C Black Ltd) – indexing, craftwork,
toy and doll-making and repairs, and pottery.

If you have brought up children you probably qualify
as a child-minder. If you have a spare room or rooms, you
might consider taking in lodgers. Have a word with the
local housing department, and your insurance company,
and get hold of a copy of the appropriate leaflet from the
Department of the Environment. You will need to master
the Rent Act, and it might be a sound idea to start with
students from your nearest college, or foreign students on
their summer holidays. This may not be much use to you
if you live in an unpicturesque part of the country, but
in any event your local tourist board ought to be helpful
with names and addresses of companies to contact.

One important inducement to taking in lodgers is that
under the 'rent a room' scheme you will be entitled to

tax relief on your profits, and the first £3250 of the annual earnings from your tenants will be free of tax entirely.

If the above possibilities are of no use to you, or your circumstances are so desperate that desperate measures are called for, you may have to think radically. You may have only one major asset to sell, your house, and that is something which deserves a chapter to itself, and is just about to get one.

8. A Very Moving Story

I have heard of a man who had a mind to sell his house, and therefore carried a piece of brick in his pocket, which he shewed as a pattern to encourage purchasers.

from The Drapier's Letters by Jonathan Swift
(No 2, 4th August, 1724)

It had been clear to me for some time that the move to a cheaper house outside Greater London would achieve a good deal to enhance our life-style. The difference between the value of our house in a leafy Home Counties suburb and the gorgeous house in East Anglia which we had set our hearts on was about £130,000. We would replace our expensive mortgage repayments with much cheaper ones, and I would be able to pay off accumulated debts at the same time. Once clear of those weighty commitments, one ought to be able to graze in the sunny pastures of well-organised finances which this book is so eloquent in promoting.

Everyone thought it to be an excellent idea. But I remained cautiously sceptical; moving house is acknowledged to be a traumatic business. Why should our experience be any different?

Anticipating trouble, my mental geiger counter identified the possible mines lying in wait for us. These were: an irregular repayment of the mortgage over the last year or so; the fact that both my wife and I are free-lancers; my own past history which consisted of periods of full employment, in which bills had been paid punctually, and periods of free-lancing in which they had not. There were to be others which the geiger counter failed to anticipate.

The good news came from the local estate agents whom we had asked to set a value on our house. The value had increased by over 20% in the past year, and they were convinced that we would have no trouble selling it. There was a great shortage of desirable houses in the area in which we lived. The phrase 'a golden post code' was tossed around. Nor was it long before we found in the unspoilt fenlands of East Anglia a house that would answer our purposes very adequately.

I said to the mortgage company: 'Great news! We're trading down. We want to replace our existing mortgage with a much smaller one, about half in fact.'

'We've been taken over,' they said.

'I know that. But my mortgage is still with you.'

'Yes, but since the take-over we are not permitted to initiate new mortgages. That has to be done through our parent company.'

'OK. I'll speak to them.'

'The trouble is that their policy is not to issue mortgages to free-lancers.'

'So, what you are telling me is that if one is finding it difficult to repay one's existing mortgage, you are not able to arrange that we should pay back one half as big. That seems crazy.'

'That's the way it is.'

For some weeks I had been receiving ugly yellow envelopes marked MG MONEYGRAM, with the insistent strap-line: IMPORTANT – OPEN IMMEDIATELY. When at length I did so the first sentence yelled in capital letters: GOOD NEWS! FIRST ALLIANCE IS PLEASED TO INFORM YOU THAT YOU HAVE BEEN PRE-QUALIFIED TO RECEIVE A HOMEOWNER LOAN FOR ANY PURPOSE.

A little further down there was a promise that there would be: NO APPLICATION FEES. NO UP-FRONT VALUATION FEES. MONEY FOR ANY PUR-POSE. *NO REPAYMENTS FOR UP TO 60 DAYS.* LOW REPAYMENTS. FAST CASH. EASY QUALIFYING. SELF-CERTIFIED INCOME OK. PLUS, EVEN IF YOU HAVE COUNTY COURT JUDGEMENTS OR CREDIT IN ARREARS, IT'S NO PROBLEM. YOU CAN GET THE MONEY YOU NEED, AND HAVE A LOW MONTHLY REPAYMENT YOU CAN AFFORD.

I thought to myself: I was not born yesterday. And then I thought: well they give a free telephone number. And then I thought: what have you to lose? And then I dialled 0800 969845.

I explained the position (after I had listened to some beastly electronic music seven times through) and was assured that there ought to be no problem. A North American First Alliance person told me that the company did not work in the fogeyish ways of their competitors, that they would be delighted to lend money to me if I were a home owner, and that they would come in a couple of days to survey the property. If then they set up an appointment for forms to be filled in and so forth we could be sure that a loan for the amount needed would be granted.

The following day I received a confirmatory call from a second executive; I would be in, would I? What was the best way to get to the house? They were looking forward to seeing me. When there was a breath taken in the monologue, I reiterated what I had explained the previous day, that I was intending to borrow money on a property I had made an offer for. Long pause. Ah. Another long pause. Hum.

'You are a home owner?'

'We've established that.'

'Am I to understand that you do not want to borrow money on your existing home?'

'In a way, I do. But it won't, I hope, be my existing home for more than a few weeks.'

'So you won't be a home owner?'

'Yes, I will. Another home.'

'But you want to borrow on this one?'

'I don't care. The purpose of the borrowing is to buy *that* one.'

'Ah. Hum. We only lend to home owners.'

The mantra had the effect of making me crosser. He continued:

'We would be happy to lend you money on your new home.'

'Good.'

'But not until you're in it. We would be delighted to do that.'

'But then I shan't need it.'

'I am so very sorry, sir. It seems we cannot accommodate you.'

A few days later I received another ugly yellow MG MONEYGRAM, and I am still receiving the beastly things. Clearly all that is gold does not necessarily glitter. It was time to talk to the bank.

Sympathetic bank staff . . .

The bank was hugely sympathetic, and when we demonstrated that the mortgage we were after was less than a third the value of the house we intended to buy and that we had received an offer for £5000 more than the asking price of our existing house, they beamed. 'We applaud your initiative. Indeed we recommended something similar to you a year ago. We shall approach a company with whom we have done some business in the past and which specialises in mortgages for the self-employed.' 'Brilliant.'

A few days later they contacted us. Not so brilliant. I had a bad credit reference, probably as a result of falling behind with the mortgage repayments. They would not be able to help. I rang a financial adviser. He was bullish. 'I don't understand the problem,' he said. 'You're free-lance? No sweat. You have a bad credit reference? So what? If you want a mortgage for less than half the value of the house, and you can show audited accounts with verifiable income for the last three years, it should be a doddle.'

When I went to see him the following morning he said it had been, if not a doddle, at least a successful search. He named the company. He gave me the forms. 'I can guarantee that they will play ball.'

But then he hit me with the figures. Because of my circumstances there would be a premium on the repayments. In the first year the repayment on the mortgage would in fact be only about 20% less than the mortgage I was currently paying, even though the mortgage was for 50% less. That couldn't be right. I went back to the bank. Would it be possible to let me have a bridging loan for the sum required for a year, after which time, and with a year's financial celibacy, it should be possible to find a mortgage. The bank considered this and announced: 'Yes.' They would be happy to do that. They would also increase my endowment cover, and ask me to declare all my current debts. Then they would lend me sufficient not just for the year's loan, but additional sums to cover the debts, and to pay the interest for the year. They would, of course, take a first charge on the new property, once it was ours.

It seemed as though the creativity of the bank and good sense had prevailed. Good sense, because anyone lending a sum of money, which is secured against a property worth a good deal more, runs no risk. The only proviso was that this offer would be subject to surveys and valuations of the properties concerned.

Then came the bombshell. The survey of our property by the putative purchasers showed that the back wall was leaning away from the roof, and that it would cost a substantial sum to correct it. They would have to pull out. We were back where we had started, except that we had spent time and money that we could ill afford.

The mystifying truth is that mortgage lenders love nothing more than lending money to a company employee. The longer he or she has worked for that company the better, and a reference from that company helps, so that if you are in regular work and wish to buy a house, or a bigger house, or increase the mortgage on an existing house, you have nothing to worry about. You can shop around and secure the best deal, interest only or endowment, fixed or variable rate. But if you are self-employed you will have to show three years' worth of audited accounts, and this is not straightforward. Many self-employed people will go to considerable lengths (or their accountants will) to earn as little taxable income as possible. There are plenty of ways in which this may be done, some of them legal, some of them less so. If you are the director of your own company, you may decide to pay yourself in dividends rather than salary. You may have started the company recently and it may be doing brilliantly, but you will only have accounts going back a year or so, and that won't help your cause. You may have considered it foolish to pay yourself much in the first years, and wise to plough money back into the company, but that won't help your cause either. If you are a writer, you may have written a book or a teleplay which is a best seller, but you know very well that that won't show up in the accounts for a good while yet. You may be acting in a sitcom, which is being bought by companies all over the world, but unless it has been on the screen for several seasons it will not show up on your magic three years of audited accounts.

One of the companies which does consider free-lance and special case mortgages – these are usually known as non-status mortgages – is UCB (UCB House, Sutton Court Road, Sutton, Surrey. Tel: 0181 401 4000), but if they are prepared to grant you a mortgage, after vetting your accounts and credit references, and finding you entirely kosher, you will still have to pay over the odds, probably about 2.25% above the standard variable rate.

There are other such companies, and an efficient mortgage broker should be able to direct you to their door. These companies are quite used to mortgage applicants with court judgements against them, and several months of arrears on their current or previous mortgage, but they like to know *why*. It will be in your favour if your problems result from a divorce, from a period of unemployment, or, if you are self-employed, from difficult trading conditions. As long as they know how you managed to get into your present mess, they are usually willing to help you to climb out of it. They turn down about one out of every three applications.

Kensington Mortgage Company (Freepost LON 3379 London. Freephone: 0800 111 020) is prepared to loan up to 80% of a property's value for a mortgage based on up to three and a half times an applicant's earnings. They claim to refuse very few who come to them, and those usually because they supply them with fraudulent information.

Inevitably there are extra charges, besides the higher interest rates, to be paid where non-status mortgages are concerned. Typically expect an application charge of about £250 and a fee on completion of about £200, along with the legal fees. Payment will have to be by direct debit, and the mortgage is likely to be dependent upon a life insurance policy, as well as a first charge on the property, of course. The life insurance element is critical because the brokers get their commissions from this part of the deal, which is why their eyes light up when they talk about insurance. It's a tough business, not for children, which reminds me that you have to be at least eighteen to be considered.

In these sort of circumstances, if you are somebody whose record is the slightest bit murky, you will need, as I have suggested, to operate through a reputable broker, but the bank may be willing to do the job for you, especially if they have a vested interest in straightening out your affairs.

There are far too many cowboys out there gunning for people like you, and it is critically important that you do not find yourself committing to a home loan which you cannot possibly service and which will thereafter result in the repossession of your house. The regulating body for mortgage brokers is the Personal Investment Authority (Hertsmere House, Hertsmere Road London, E14. Tel: 0171 538 8860, or 103 New Oxford Street, London W1. Tel: 0171 379 0444). If the broker you are dealing with is not a member, I suggest that you get out of the office pretty damn quick.

This business of credit references requires a few paragraphs, because a bad credit reference, once acquired, is as hard to get rid of as a branded A on the forehead of an adulterer. Increasingly we live in a world where credit is king. The delayed payment of a telephone bill is probably not too serious, but mortgage payments delayed over more than three months lead to a very black mark indeed, and this may have knock-on effects which you had not anticipated. Apart from problems in remortgaging, it may not be possible to buy a car – except for cash – or anything much else worth having.

So how do you get rid of a bad credit reference, or how establish whether the one in your name is all a terrible mistake? It happens, although not as often as the victim thinks it has happened.

There are two main credit reference agencies, Experian (which used to be called CCN) and Equifax. These are their addresses: Experian, PO BOX 40, Nottingham NG7 2SS. Tel: 0115 941 0888; Equifax Europe UK Ltd, PO Box 3001, Glasgow G81 2DT. Tel: 01274 759 759.

These companies store information on everyone on the electoral roll, as well as detailed information on credit agreements, repayment patterns, and arrears. If you have defaulted or been in arrears on your mortgage they will know it. If you have fallen behind with hire purchase agreements or personal loans they will know it. If you have been successfully sued by a builder or plumber for money owing, they will know that too. They probably know more about you than your doctor, spouse, near relations, priest, rabbi, or imam put together. Fortunately there is a lifeline available to you. Under the Data Protection Act 1984, you have certain rights. If you have been turned down for credit as a result of a bad credit reference, the company which has turned you down is obliged by law to tell you the source of the information which has led them to be so unhelpful. Once you know which credit reference has been used, send them a cheque or postal order for £1, your name and addresses and post codes for the past six years, and they are obliged to let you have all the information about you which they are keeping on their files.

One of the most unfair aspects of what is a heartless business is that you may have a lousy credit reference, merely because of a failed business, run by your husband or wife. You ought to be circumspect, therefore, if you are asked to guarantee a loan to support a partner's business. If it fails your credit reference will be wrecked. You could even lose your house or be made bankrupt. But how do you say 'No' to a request like this from somebody you love?

The official who is on your side in these matters is the Data Protection Registrar (Wycliffe House, Water Lane, Wilmslow, Cheshire SK9 5AF. Tel: 01625 545 700) and the Registrar has published two leaflets: *Using the Law to Protect your Information* and *You and your Credit File.* They are free on application.

There are companies which specialise in a comparatively new kind of business, which is known as Credit Repair. You will find them advertising widely in the tabloid press and in the pages of *Exchange and Mart*, *Loot*, and so forth. They make ambitious claims. 'CCJs and Defaults Legally Removed!' they trumpet. 'We can help you with Credit Repair Service/Bank Accounts/Personal Finance/Loans and Mortgages/Business Bank Accounts/ Contract Car Hire,' they boast. One almost wants to ask them: can they guarantee life after death?

On your behalf I contacted a couple of them to find out the nature of the service they offer.

Eagle Enterprise (MIC House, 1–3 Grant Road, London SW11 2NU. Tel: 0171 223 4788) is licensed by the Office of Fair Trading (Licence number: 166965) which is encouraging. They sent me a yellow letter and a pale blue form and a pale green form. The yellow letter explained the nature of the services on offer, and advised that the removal/repair of adverse information takes between three and six weeks 'but can take longer in difficult or complex cases'. The *Credit Repair Service* ('in short we do the work, and you just have to sign your name!') costs a one-off £65, although if you reply within fourteen days there is a discount of £20. There appeared not to be a money-back guarantee on this or the gold service. This *Gold Service* involves a one-off fee of £95 ('save £30.00!! if you reply within fourteen days') and offers, in addition to the full repair service, 'a personal written report on your file for the purpose of ensuring the high credit score necessary to guarantee passing credit checks for the following: A. Mortgages, B. Credit Cards, C. Car Finance, D. Loans. Don't delay, Act today!' was the cry, with the additional sweetener that if you sent off your £95 less £30 you would also receive a copy of '*Credit Secrets and Finance Handbook* (this very informative publication retails at £22.99)'.

The pale green form contained on the back the terms and conditions imposed by Eagle Enterprise. By signing, you were committing yourself (and I paraphrase the document for brevity): to co-operate fully, and to respond quickly and accurately, and to pass on any documents you may receive; to give full consent to Eagle Enterprise to act as Credit Repair Specialists and to make unlimited inquiries; to acknowledge that the work must always comply with the laws of England; that any business decision affecting the applicant may depend on information provided by third parties 'whose accuracy Eagle Enterprise cannot control'; that Eagle shall in no circumstances be liable for any loss suffered by the applicant as a result of its inquiries; that the applicant will indemnify Eagle against any claim or action made against them as a result of their inquiries; and that in any event Eagle will not be liable for any loss 'whether arising out of negligence of Eagle Enterprise . . . or otherwise'. Ouch! I was not entirely enamoured of that pale green form.

The pale blue form, which did carry a 'money-back guarantee – no credit checks' offered various services including:

1. A UK personal account with 'a major high street bank *without searching your past credit history'*. Application costs £60. Three weeks to process.
2. A UK Offshore Personal Gold account requiring an initial deposit of £250 or more but providing a cheque guarantee card with a Visa/Delta Debit Card, and other bits and pieces. Application costs £250. Six weeks to process. Copy of passport, witnessed by bank manager or solicitor required and various other documents.
3. Guaranteed loan service for home owners and tenants of up to £15,000. Ring for details. Application costs £250. Four weeks to process.
4. Mortgages and remortgages status and non-status. Ring for details. Initial application costs £50. Time of processing varies.

5. Business accounts. Ring for details. Application costs £350.
6. Contract Car Hire. Ring for details. Application costs £350.

   I am afraid to report that I put the pale blue form where I put the pale green form.

   The letter from AGC Associates (Cairns House, 2 Cairns Road, Battersea, London SW11 1ES), Credit Repair Specialists, is a triumph of understatement. They suggest that the reason you have been in touch with them is that you may have been refused credit and 'as a result suffered some embarrassment or inconvenience'. Yes. They add that 'there is usually one key reason why some people are repeatedly turned down for credit. It is because they have County Court Judgements, defaults, or other bad credit information registered against their name or their address.' Well, again yes. They acknowledge that there are two million such unfortunates in the UK, and explain that bad credit information remains on the files for AT LEAST SIX YEARS even if the debt has been paid off. The capital letters cry out passionately from the page. They then assure you that by using the credit repair process over 50,000 people have successfully improved their rating during the last year alone.

   What they do is identify the negative information against you by the credit agencies (which of course you can do yourself on payment of £1 – see above), and 'allow you to have it completely removed from the record'. AGC claims that this procedure has proved successful for 'over 95% of our clients', that the total cost of the Repair Service is just £35 (for any number of CCJs and defaults). They add that, if they fail, they offer a **FULL MONEY BACK GUARANTEE** (this deserves, it seems, not just capital letters but bold type as well). They promise confidentiality, and suggest that if you subscribe £35 you are entitled to purchase *The Complete Credit Secrets & Finance Handbook* for a special price of £9.95 (normally £18.95).

I rang their free advice line (02181 771 6894), and asked them how they go about it. Do they hack into the credit company computers? The agreeable young man was appalled at the suggestion, although he did concede that some of their competitors might give that impression in some of their advertising. 'It would be illegal,' he said, 'and near impossible.' The adjective worried me. What AGC does, he said, was negotiate with the companies in whose black books you find yourself, and let you know what you need to pay them in return for having the bad reference excised. It may be easier to do this when amounts are outstanding, rather than when they have been paid off. Clearly those to whom you owe money will be more anxious to help you out in return for settlement than those to whom you don't.

So where did I go wrong in my panicked attempt to get a mortgage, and the disastrous survey? With hindsight it is easy to judge that I should have obtained a mortgage in principle *before* putting my house on the market and making an offer for another one; and paid for a survey to be done in advance too. But it is so often the way that when you are in dire financial straits you cut corners, and it is people in these straits who can least afford to do so.

But I can report that thanks to the bank's good offices

(why be coy? The bank was Lloyd's and the manager's name was – but he asked me not to name him and so I won't – OK, Tony?) we were able to buy our house in the country, and very fine it is too. But I have to report another trap into which I fell, and which you must guard against with your life.

When the time came for us to move I asked three companies, all members of the Guild of Removers and Storers, to quote for the job. One quoted at £3600, one £2600, and one £1600. At which moment I forgot that John Ruskin had warned that you should never take the lowest estimate for anything, because while you *might* save a little money, you *could* lose everything. Our removers turned out to be both greedy and incompetent, and we ended up having to pay them over £6000 before they would tell us where our furniture was being stored, or indeed agree to release it. At the time of writing I have taken out a summons against them in the Small Claims Court. And the Guild? So far, quite unhelpful. The moral is: Get everything in writing. Study it. And don't let anyone have access to your credit card number.

A final word about the whole business of mortgages. There has been a flurry of interest recently in what has become known as the Australian System. This apparently simple and sensible idea is that some mortgage companies (AIB, Bank of Scotland Mortgage Direct, Clydesdale, Darlington Building Society, Direct Line, Dudley Building Society, First Direct, Furness Building Society, Legal and General MSL, Midland, Mortgage Trust, The Mortgage Business, National Bank of Australia, Northern Bank (Northern Ireland), Royal Bank of Scotland, Scottish Widows Bank, Sun Banking Corporation, and Yorkshire Bank) calculate the interest on your repayment mortgage – the system only applies to repayment mortgages – on a daily basis, instead of a monthly or annual basis. Every time you pay money into your mortgage account, the interest is adjusted accordingly. The results are electrifying. On a Nationwide twenty-five year mortgage of £115,000, the savings would be £8343 (at present interest rates) and the twenty-five year debt would be paid off ten months early. If you are able to increase your monthly repayments, the savings are even more astronomical. Were you able to increase them by £50, the savings on a £200,000 mortgage would be £81,585 and the twenty-five year term would be cut to just seventeen. Even on a £50,000 mortgage the saving would be a tasty £4448.

A few companies offer monthly adjustable ('flexible') mortgages. These are the Market Harborough Building Society, Stroud and Swindon Building Society, and the Tipton and Coseley Building Society.

Such has been the publicity given to the staggering savings claimed by those who offer the Australian System that the banks have been forced to consider the technique as it might apply to their existing clients; the building societies less so, as they are deeply rooted in the monthly tradition. So those who have a vested interest in the traditional methods point out that 8% paid daily is *not* cheaper than 7% paid monthly. But two conclusions may fairly be drawn. The first that, until the daily interest payments idea was initiated, those offering mortgages adjusted monthly or yearly were making an inordinate amount of profit. The second that it is at least worth asking whether the company through whom you are paying your mortgage operates a daily interest system, and, if not, why not? Should you decide to move to a bank which does offer the Australian System, you may well have to pay your existing company a penalty, although many penalties only apply if you are moving your custom after less than five years.

Increasingly when interest rates are moving up home-owners get desperate for fixed interest mortgages, which have at least the advantage of letting you know what you are going to have to pay in advance. It's a critical decision, and one which everyone must decide for themselves. But if you believe rates will continue to rise you should go for fixed interest. Currently the banks and building societies offering these mortgages which can be safely recommended are:

Mortgages with rates fixed for two years

Abbey National
Bristol and West
Chelsea Building Society
First Mortgage
Lambeth Building Society*
Skipton Building Society*
Woolwich

These require you also to take out an insurance policy with them.

Mortgages with rates fixed for three years

Abbey National
Bristol and West

Cheshire Building Society
First Mortgage
Halifax
Lambeth Building Society
Newcastle Building Society

Mortgages with rates fixed for five years

Bristol and West
Lambeth Building Society
Nationwide Building Society
Newcastle Building Society
Northern Rock Building Society
Principality Building Society
Prudential Banking

There are numerous other forms of mortgages – variable rate, low start, capital and interest repayment, endowment, pension, PEP, and discounted mortgages – about which vast books could be written (and certainly have been) but if you are to get through this chapter by bedtime I shall leave it there, with just one worrying thought to keep you awake.

How do you know whether you are paying the correct amount into your mortgage account? You probably don't, and since many top banks and building societies do not let you have the information you need in order to make this calculation, it's no wonder.

They ought to. *The Mortgage and Banking Code* is supposed to be given to all customers, but often is not. Many banks and building society staff don't even know about it. In which case they almost certainly don't know about the recently published *Code of Mortgage Lending Practice*, and since this is the document which helps the Mortgage Ombudsman make his/her judgements, it ought not to be a secret. Ask for both documents, and if your proposed mortgage company doesn't have a copy of both or either, ask why not.

In the meantime, and on the assumption that you have been able to get hold of the relevant facts and figures here is the equation which will enable you to work out whether you are being charged the right amount of mortgage repayment.

THE SITUATION

The start of the year balance on your mortgage account: £55,000; MIRAS at 15% on the first £30,000: £4500.

a) Interest rates 1st Jan – 31st July: 7.99%
b) Interest rates 1st Aug – to 31st Dec: 8.49%

NB Currently MIRAS is 15%, but from April 1998 it reduces to 10%.

HOW TO WORK OUT THE INTEREST

	£
a) Jan – July interest:	
£30,000 (MIRAS element) ×7.99% ×85% (MIRAS deducted) divided by 365 (to give the daily interest) ×212 (which is the number of days for which 7.99 is charged)	1183.40
£25,000 (non MIRAS element) ×7.99 divided by 365 ×212	1160.19
Total of interest due for Jan – July	2343.59

b) Aug – Dec interest: £
   £30,000 ×8.49 ×85% divided by 365 ×153 days 907.50
   £25,000 ×8.40 divided by 365 ×153   889.71
Total of interest due for Aug – Dec   1797.21

Total for the year a) + b)   4140.80

If you find that you have been charged more than
you think you should have been, it is quite possible
that you have been punished for being in arrears with
your payments. These arrears may be punitive, and you
may find an extra hoick of 1% on your interest rates
for those months in which you have fallen behind. The
Ombudsman will rule, if necessary, on whether or not
you are being justly fined).

I cannot understand why they do not teach such things
at school.

9. Money for Nothing – Get your Kicks for Free

For even honest men may act like sinners
Unless they've had their customary dinners.

from *The Threepenny Opera* by Bertolt Brecht,
trans. Marc Blitzstein

I thought long and hard about whether or not to include this chapter. It is a difficult subject to deal with. But since it is one which might get some of those who read this book into *very* serious difficulties (although it just might get some out of them), I thought I would; so I have.

First, then, a confession. I was once quite without money or any means in the short-term of getting hold of any. I was living away from home at a college, where I was fed and watered, so I was not going hungry, but I was on my way home for the week-end – by bus – to see my wife and small children. I had this urge to take the children a present. Nothing much; just something to assure them that I had been thinking of them. I went into W.H. Smith and stole two small toys.

It is confusing, do you not find, when the moral imperatives of a lifetime clash with the instincts of parenthood? Put less pompously, have you ever done anything like that yourself? Or been tempted to? If you have not then you might quite safely skip to the next chapter. But it is my belief that a majority of the impoverished *do* fantasise about theft or fraud or other dishonest ways of making a fast buck.

I have also been on the receiving end. When running a stall or a shop I have had items stolen from me, and seen other stallholders in great distress when items were stolen from them. Once I had a tiny Wedgwood saucer lifted from a display counter; they left me the matching cup, which I could no longer look at with any pleasure. On another occasion, a most amiable woman had her moneybelt stolen, with the complete day's takings in it, and was in tears.

We are not always set good examples, are we? One reads that the big chains write off a percentage of their profits, because they know that shop-lifting occurs, and it is cheaper and easier to write it off, than to employ suffi-cient security staff to monitor the shops. One knows, too, that most establishments pay heavy insurance premiums, so that if they lose large amounts, they can claim them back. This makes it easy for the criminal to argue: 'Well, what's it matter if the insurance pays anyway?' The truth is that everyone pays through a premium on the prices of the goods charged, this being a levy to cover the cost of insurance, or greater vigilance, or both.

It is also discouraging to the honest citizen to read that Sir Useless Fat Cat, who has recently been discharged from his position as a Director of Lovely Big Bucks Ltd, is being paid a golden handshake equivalent to two and a half times his annual salary in return for going quietly. Or that the Minister in Charge of the Privatisation of the Air we Breathe, having lost his job, is now being employed by the Air We Breathe Company which is convinced that the contacts he has established in such a long and extinguished career, will be of the greatest benefit to them; and that the salary he is being paid adds up to an awful lot of Ks, just as his not terribly honourable discharge as a Minister of the Crown left him not exactly skint.

How is one to cope with these double standards? The best way I can is to remember what the stallholder next to me at Trash and Treasure Antiques Market in Cookham Church Hall said to me after I reported the painful theft of a Treasure rather than a piece of Trash. 'You will get over it,' this very wise woman said, 'but whoever took it will have to live with it always.' I doubt, however, whether Sir Useless Fat Cat or the Ex-Minister suffers too many sleepless nights contemplating his ill-merited affluence.

There used to be a small branch of Barclays Bank in St Margarets, Twickenham. It was one of the last branches to be modernised and still had grilles in place of bullet-proof glass. Sometimes when I went in there to cash my cheque for £30, I thought that anyone with a bit of nerve, no moral sense, and a halfway convincing toy gun, could walk out with the contents of the tills, just like that, as dear Tommy Cooper used to say. Then one day they did. And the next day, predictably, men with drills and large sheets of plate-glass moved in.

When the chips are down, the attractions of the lottery, scratch cards and similar indulgences are not easy to resist. Advertisers are clever people and the massive inducements of 'It Could Be You!' have not only raised false hopes in gullible people, they have led them to

spend a little of what little they have to buy the Churchill Papers for the nation. I mean!

(I am advised that you should never buy a lottery ticket for the Saturday draw on a Monday, as you are far more likely to die during the week than to win a major prize. Nor should you cross a road to a newsagent to buy a ticket, since you are more likely to be knocked down by a car than to win the jackpot. You are more likely to be struck by lightning than to win, and I should know, since I have been struck by lightning.)

So, what about gambling? Here, to be frank, I have a dilemma. When I am not writing books about the money running out, I am writing a racing system which, twice a year, encourages its subscribers to believe that they have every chance of becoming massively rich. Some of them write and tell me how massively rich they have become thanks to following the System. Some don't. But supposing you bought it and for some mystifying reason failed to become rich? How do you suppose I would feel then? This is why I am not even going to give you the name of the System, nor how much it costs, nor where you can get hold of a copy, nor how wonderful it is. That's the sort of bloke I am.

But for people who see the chasm opening up in front of them, gambling is a serious temptation. There is an anecdote in Evelyn Waugh's diaries, when he describes a visit to the tables at Monte Carlo, in the days when Monte Carlo was very glamorous indeed. (It's mainly fruit machines now.) An oil sheikh approaches the table and tells the croupier that he wants to gamble, but

will only do so if the maximum limits on the table are removed. The croupier goes off to see the *chef du casino*, and asks: 'What should I do?' The wise old *chef du casino* says: 'Is he sitting down or standing up, our gambling-mad sheikh?' 'Sitting down,' says the croupier. 'Why then, no limits,' says the *chef*. This is because he is confident that if the sheikh is sitting down he intends to spend some time at the table, and that if he spends some time at the table the odds in the house's favour will ensure that he loses. What a casino could not cope with would be an oil sheikh putting down $50 million on an even chance, winning, and walking away.

It is romantic to think that, when you do your sums and find that you have £6000 in the world and debts of £7000 demanding to be paid, a single bet at even money will give you a chance to get straight. It's true; it will. But it will take a bit of organising. For one thing how do you convert your £6000 of assets into ready money which you can hold in your hot hand and pass into the even hotter one of the bookmaker? And, having done so, how do you choose where to risk it? In most horse-races the odds reflect a percentage of about 14% in favour of the layers. This means that if one hundred people decide to go down the route of putting their last five grand on a horse, fifty-seven of them are likely to go home skint, and only forty-three in a taxi. (I hope they have all had the sense to make their bet on a racecourse, thus avoiding paying the current 9% tax on all bets struck off course.)

You may point out, sagely, that in a casino where the roulette wheel has just the one nought, if the same one hundred people put their cash onto one of the even chances, about forty-seven of them would go home in

a taxi, but how are you going to find a casino prepared
to take your £5000, and, if you do, what about the money
you will have to put down for membership, acceptable
clothes and suchlike? What I suspect we are talking
about here is a reluctance to accept the responsibility for
one's own fate. If, runs the argument, I am going to sink
without trace, I want to be able to gasp from the gutter: 'At
least it was not my fault.' It may be romantic, but there is
not very much dignity in such an approach to life.

Before dismissing the gambling option let me write
another sentence or two about why it will not be a way
out of your troubles. Let us suppose you are able to find
a winning horse and that your £5000 debts are wiped off
at a stroke. It may happen, but probably won't. You will
feel great about it for a while, and then you will begin to
consider that if you could do it once, why not a second
time? All you have to do is find another horse at even
money, and so forth. Tragic. Horses, as they say, don't
bet on people.

10. I'll Huff and I'll Puff and I'll Blow your House Down

Sir Richard Steele having one day invited to his house a great number of persons of the first quality, they were surprised at the number of liveries which surrounded the table; and after dinner, when wine and mirth had set them free from the observation of rigid ceremony, one of them inquired of Sir Richard how such an expensive train of domestics could be consistent with his fortune. Sir Richard very frankly confessed that they were fellows of whom he would very willingly be rid. And being then asked why he did not discharge them, declared that they were bailiffs who had introduced themselves with an execution, and whom, since he could not send them away, he had thought it convenient to embellish with liveries that they might do him credit while they stayed.

from *Lives* by Samuel Johnson

For notes on Scottish procedure, see the end of this chapter.

Proceedings for debts take place in civil courts, usually the county courts, very occasionally the High Court. County court cases are geared to the modest citizen, who will not normally be represented by counsel, and are presided over by registrars. It is unlikely that the newspapers will interest themselves in the proceedings, and the atmosphere is not calculated to inspire terror or alarm.

In cases where the sums involved are substantial, a writ may arrive from the High Court, and you would be well advised to contact a solicitor as a matter of some urgency. Apart from other considerations, you have just two weeks to respond.

The traditional sequence for modest defaults and arrears is this:

1. The Creditor, who is now the Plaintiff, issues a default summons (form **N1**).
2. a) You, the Debtor, who are now the defendant, do not admit liability, in which case you should consult a solicitor, or visit the CAB, or a law centre, to organise your defence.

   b) You do admit liability, and return form **N9A**, admitting the debt and making an offer to pay.

   c) You dispute the amount or make a counterclaim. In this case you need to fill in and return form **9B**.

   d) You ignore the summons, in which case the Plaintiff requests the court that a judgement be entered, and there's no reason why the Registrar should say No.
3. If you follow the course under 2 b) and admit liability and make an offer to pay, two consequences may follow:

   a) The Plaintiff may accept your offer. Then there will be Judgement by Consent, an order for Payment by Consent, which may be in full or by instalments, and you should request an Administration Order Form

N92, and fill it out giving details of all relevant debts. If you then pay in full or keep up the payments of the instalments, there need be no further action.

b) If the Plaintiff does not accept your offer, there will be a hearing and the Registrar will make an Order for Payment, which will also be entered on the ubiquitous **N92**.

4. What happens if you can't or won't or don't pay in full? You will need to fill in **N245**, asking for further time to pay, or a reduction in the instalments, incorporated in a revised offer. Then:

a) The Plaintiff may accept your offer, in which case there will be a new instalment order by consent.

b) The Plaintiff does not accept your offer. There will have to be another court hearing, with the Registrar making further arrangements for you to pay, with an Order for Payment.

5. But if you don't apply for further time to pay, the Plaintiff can then apply for:

a) a Charging Order, which the courts will either grant or dismiss.

What does a Charging Order do? It gives the creditor security for the debt, which then becomes enforceable on a property, the way a mortgage does. A Charging Order Nisi (nisi is Latin for unless) means that the court accepts that you own or part own the property, which is the subject of the Charging Order. You will be sent a copy of the Nisi with seven days notice – at least – of a hearing in front of a District Judge. During these seven days you are not allowed to sell the property. At the next hearing a decision will be taken on whether or not to make a permanent charge (a Charging Absolute) on your property. If you don't turn up in court for this hearing – you really ought to – the judge will probably grant the abominable Absolute. If you can't manage the date, contact the court for a date you can cope with. There are then several lines of defence which you can try, as follows:

i)   Illness in the family.

ii)   Other creditors who might have prior claims.

iii)   The debt is insignificantly small in comparison with the value of your house.

iv)   If you are in employment you could suggest that an Attachment of Earnings Order (that means a series of payments taken directly from your wage packet) might answer the case.

v)   Negative equity in the property.

vi)   You are likely to be made bankrupt.

vii)   The Charging Order could sensibly be subsumed within an Administration Order.

viii) Exceptional hardship for your family will result.

ix)   You are involved in divorce or separation proceedings.

x)   You own the property jointly but the debt is only in your name.

NB It's unusual for an Order for Sale of your home to be made through these means, but the legal procedures are complicated, so a visit to your local CAB, or a call to the National Debtline (0645 500 511) is strongly advised.

b) a Garnishee Order. This is a request to anyone who holds the debtor's assets (a bank or an insurance endowment company, for instance) to hand them over to the Plaintiff.

c) an Oral Examination. This you are required to attend and your income and assets will be assessed publicly, before the Registrar decides what is best to do.

d) an Attachment of Earnings. You will then have to fill in an **N56**, showing details of your income and spending patterns. This Attachment may be granted, suspended, or refused. If it's granted, your employer – if you have one – will be instructed to hand over your earnings.

e) a Warrant of Execution. I'm afraid to say that this is the most likely course, and it will bring in those least popular of God's creatures, after possibly traffic wardens, the bailiffs.

The bailiffs have no right to come into your house. They can knock and ring until they are purple in the face, but, *unless they have been in your house before*, there is no obligation upon you to open the door. Nor must they break in. Nor must they invite the police to help them break in – at least they can, but the police won't. The police will only interest themselves if a breach of the peace is likely to be caused.

You must be very clear that bailiffs cannot seize goods without going through the proper procedures. They cannot (though they may think they can) put a notice through your door telling you that all your goods, or some of them, are being levied. If they don't come into the house, they are not allowed to take anything away from it.

And this important proviso applies as much to walking possession as to distraint. Nor must you sign a walking possession order on behalf of someone else.

I repeat: Don't let the bailiffs into the house if you can possibly help it! If you have a reason to expect them to call, keep your doors locked and your windows secured. They will try to get you to open the door and push past you. They mustn't. They may shout through the door that they are desperate to use the loo; tell them to go away. If they telephone to say they would like to come and see you for a chat, tell them that you have taken a vow of silence.

If you offer them a part payment or a payment over a period of time and they accept, go outside to pay them, securing your door. Get a receipt. And don't sign anything they give you to sign.

6. Once the Warrant of Execution has been granted, the bailiffs come to call. It is just possible that they will find nothing of value, and will return the Warrant to the court marked 'no goods'.

    Far more likely, though, is that they will find stuff worth selling, and they will make a list of goods to the value of the outstanding debt. Of course they are not the most knowledgeable of men, and I have had occasion to point out to them the difference between the 18th and 19th century, and between walnut and mahogany! Once the list has been drawn up, a copy will be handed to you, and, although the items will not at that time be removed, the bailiffs will have 'walking possession' of them.

    If you have a car, whose value more than covers

the cost of the debts, the easiest and least painful procedure is to suggest that the car be put down against the debt; you can still keep it and drive it, of course, but you will lose it if the debt is not satisfied when it is supposed to be.

It is also possible, if you are unlucky, or if the bailiffs are in a lousy mood, that they will 'impound' your goods, which means taking them away. You must insist that they have no rights over anything *which did not belong to you at the time the Warrant of Execution was passed through the courts.*

They may try to remove items which don't belong to you, and you must not permit this. Tell them that if they insist on removing goods which they are not entitled to, because of queries of ownership, or because they are still the subject of a hire purchase agreement – or any other reason – you must draw up your own inventory and tell them that they will be liable for costs if any of the items is improperly removed. You should then have the inventory drawn up as a Statutory Declaration and signed by the owner and debtor in the presence of a Commissioner of Oaths (this is something most high street solicitors can undertake cheaply and quickly). If you can show that the goods have been wrongly seized you can then apply for an injunction to have them returned to their proper owner.

There are some things which bailiffs must never take. 'Fixtures and fittings' are exempt, though this may be subject to interpretation. Light fittings and kitchen units ought to stay, although light shades and shelf units could go. The law also requires that the bailiffs leave you: 'such clothing, bedding, furniture, household equipment and provisions as are necessary for satisfying the basic domestic needs of that person and his family; such tools, goods, vehicles and other items of equipment as are necessary to that person for use personally by him in his employment, business or vocation.' This sounds all very fine and dandy but how this instruction is interpreted may be down to the county court bailiffs themselves.

What happens to the goods which the bailiffs seize? They are sold at public auction, and often fetch a tiny percentage of their true worth. If you have been able to raise a bit of money before the auction (which may be as soon as five days after seizure) you have a chance of buying your treasures back. Ask the bailiffs to let you know when and where the goods are to be sold.

7. When the bailiffs have done their worst, you still have alternative courses of action:

    a) You can pay the amount on the warrant plus costs, the 'walking possession' will be returned to you, and you can resume your life as if nothing has happened.
    b) You can apply for a suspension of the warrant (form **N245**) and make a new instalment offer. This the Plaintiff may accept, giving you a bit more breathing space. If the Plaintiff refuses, the court will fix a hearing once more and the Registrar will decide whether to suspend the warrant or not.

Although bailiffs, like traffic wardens, are, I suppose,

God's children, they have been known to behave improperly. You may complain to the court which instructed them. I complained once that bailiffs who send out warning letters, with five working days' notice, should not send them out by second class post. Clearly the reason they were doing so was in the hope that the customer would fail to respond in time. The bailiff makes more money by the selling of goods than by the preliminary routines. For the same reason, I suspect, that particular firm, made sure that it was impossible to get through to them by telephone. Disgraceful.

You also have the right to complain to any trade organisation of which the bailiffs may be members, to the local authority (if it is the Creditor) or to the Parliamentary Ombudsman.

Bailiffs' charges are as follows: for visiting your home and not getting in: £15 for the first visit, £12.50 for the second; for making a list of goods for distraint: 15% of the value for the first £100, or part of it, 4% from £100 to £500, 2.5% from £500 to £2000; for removing and storing your possessions: 'reasonable costs'.

It would be an exaggeration to suggest that the legislature is on your side when you run into debt, but it is not entirely heartless. Section 40 of the Administration of Justice Act, for instance, protects the Debtor from harassment by the Creditor, if demands for payment are 'in respect of their frequency, or the manner or occasion of making any such demand, or of any threat or publicity by which any demand is accompanied, calculated to subject him or members of his family or household to alarm, distress or humiliation', or if the Creditor falsely suggests that criminal proceedings will result from your failure to pay, or if the Creditor produces a document which (s)he claims to be official when it isn't. In short they must not make your life a misery, or utter false threats.

Some things they may try: pretend to be a court official; contact your boss and cause embarrassment; leave a van outside your house marked in big, red letters: DEBT COLLECTORS; pester your neighbours; take your benefits book.

So what can you do about it?

a) Write to them, quote Section 40 of the Act, and tell them to mend their ways.

b) If they don't, complain to the Trading Standards or Consumer Protection Department of your friendly local council.

c) If you still have no joy, try the Office of Fair Trading.

d) And you could always have a go at any trade association of which your creditor is a member. If they do belong to some professional body they will probably carry their logo boastfully at the top of their literature.

e) You may prosecute in a Magistrates' Court, but it could cost you. If you've received any letter from the Creditor which is indecent or grossly offensive or threatening or which contains deliberately false information, you may well have a solid case for prosecution. Check with your Citizens Advice Bureau.

To finish a gloomy chapter on an upbeat note. One of the things bailiffs cannot do is send you to prison. Furthermore, if they fail to get into your house, and won't accept your offer of part payment, all they can do is refer things back to the council who employed them.

NOTES ON SCOTTISH PROCEDURE

In Scotland some of the terms are different. County Courts are Sheriff Courts; Default Summons is Small Claims Summons up to £750 and Summary Cause Summons between £750 and £1,500; Plaintiff is Pursuer; Registrar is Sheriff.

The Pursuer completes a Small Claims Form and sends it to the court. You will receive a copy of this document with a return date marked on it. You must reply by the return date if you wish to defend the action or if you wish to apply for a Time to Pay Direction. If you admit the claim and wish to pay by instalments you should complete Box 1 and Section B, remembering to fill in the amount you can pay per week. Alternatively, you can admit the claim and, if you wish to go to court, to agree the payments you should complete Box 2. If you deny the claim you should complete Box 3. Since a Time To Pay Direction will spoil your credit reference, it's preferable to come to a private agreement with the Pursuer if you can.

Summary Cause procedures are similar but higher expenses can be awarded against you. If the claim is admitted, or denied but found in favour of the Pursuer, decree judgement will be awarded against you on the hearing date. If a Time to Pay Direction is awarded then no further action is likely by the Pursuer provided that you keep to the repayment schedule. If you fail to keep up with the payments (by two instalments when the third is due) or if no Time to Pay Direction is granted then the Pursuer can issue a Charge for Payment which allows you fourteen days to settle in full. If no payment is made within this period the Pursuer can petition for your sequestration (bankruptcy) if the debt is more than £1,500 or can instruct Sheriff Officers to poind (effectively seize) your moveable assets to the value of the decree regardless of the amount of the claim. These assets are likely to be sold at auction. During the next fourteen days you are entitled to redeem any article at the value fixed on the poinding schedule. It should be noted that a second poinding cannot be executed on the same premises under the same decree on the instructions of the same Creditor unless you have brought further poindable goods into the premises. The Pursuer can apply for an earnings arrestment if he feels that you are in a position to make regular contributions from your earnings. The Sheriff will make an appropriate order after considering the issue and asking you for details of your income and expenditure. The Sheriff can freeze your bank account at any time after the Pursuer has lodged his/her claim with the court, but only if there's money in it (which there probably isn't!).

The items which are excluded from poinding include clothing, tools of trade, books for household education, toys and child care articles, household belongings such as beds, tables, food, curtains, floor coverings, cooking utensils, fridges, tools for maintenance and furniture for storing these items.

11.   After Noise, Tranquillity

Asked in Leigh today if he could pay a 20s fine and two guinea costs for maliciously wounding his wife with a poker, a man replied: 'You will have to ask the missus. I have no money.'

Manchester Evening News

For notes on Scottish procedure, see the end of this chapter.

A word of warning about this chapter. Bankruptcy is a technical business. Even if you are only considering it, or if someone is considering petitioning you for it, you must take advice, initially from your Citizens Advice Bureau. Why from them initially? Because the advice is free, confidential, impartial, and likely to be sensible.

Now I can go ahead and write the chapter, relieved that you won't be jeopardising your future merely as a result of a few sentences written by me.

Bankruptcy is a word deriving from Holland where the breaking of a bench was the sign that a money-lender was no longer solvent. It sounds horrible, and for most bankrupts it is horrible, but there are some cases where it remains the preferred option. It is also a way – the only way, barring death or time-travel – of having your debts written off.

How can it be the preferred option? If, for instance, you

have debts which you cannot pay, you are not working and do not intend to work again, you are a tenant and have no wish to own your own house, and you don't care tuppence about your credit-rating, bankruptcy could be a very satisfactory way out of your difficulties. For most other people, it isn't. But preferred? Very possibly.

For bankruptcy usually means that you will pay less than you would otherwise have to. It does give you the chance of a fresh start. It may mean that you are discharged within three years, while a more sophisticated option may drag on for much longer. Your creditors know where they stand, and so do you, and once you have been discharged, your debts will be written off. Well not quite all of them, in fact. Secured creditors, fines, maintenance and court orders, debts from personal injury claims, and debts incurred through fraud, will not be written off.

You can petition the county court (or, in London, the High Court) on your own behalf. This is done using form **6.27**, together with an affidavit and a statement of your affairs, set out on form **6.28**. Inevitably you will also have to send some money. Currently the court fee is £50 and the deposit £250. Where you get this £250 from is an excellent question, since the reason for petitioning for bankruptcy is that you have no money. But the Citizens Advice Bureau ought to be your first port of call.

Once it has been agreed that you are to petition for bankruptcy, you must withdraw all that you can from bank and building society accounts before the petition goes to court, so that you have something to live on.

The forms are complicated, and you will need the help of a debt adviser – probably from the CAB – to complete them. All creditors and all debts will have to be included, with an estimate of the value of your possessions – this is based on the money they would be likely to fetch at auction, not the replacement or insurance value. If a creditor has a prior claim on any of these possessions, that will have to be noted, because they will belong to the creditor not the Official Receiver. The same with any existing actions being pursued against you in the courts. Also you will have to put down any income that you may have.

If your debts are less than £20,000 (1992), and your assets at least £2000, and if you haven't been the subject of bankruptcy proceedings in the last five years the court may decide that an Individual Voluntary Arrangement (IVA, see below) is more appropriate in your case. But if you don't want one, you will have to tell the court that you don't and why.

These are the possible outcomes to the petition. An IVA may be granted, a bankruptcy order may be granted or dismissed, the proceedings adjourned or stayed. You will forgive me if I don't detail the implications of these outcomes more fully.

A creditor or a group of creditors can petition for you to be made bankrupt, but under the Insolvency Act 1985 this can only happen when your debts to that or those creditor(s) amount to at least £750 (£1500 in Scotland). It will cost the petitioners £200 to get you to the Official Receiver in Bankruptcy. They will first have to serve a Statutory Demand on you; if there is evidence that you are unable to pay, the creditors through the county court will be able to pursue you with a Petition for Bankruptcy. The Statutory Demand, which has to be served directly on a debtor, requires you to pay what's demanded, or secure it against property, or offer to repay it by instalments,

I'd never realised how many people took The London Gazette –

the offer having to be acceptable to the creditor(s). You have twenty-one days after the Statutory Demand before the bankruptcy proceedings can be instituted, and if, during that time, you can reduce the debt to below £750, you cannot be made bankrupt. All bankruptcies are advertised in *The London Gazette*.

If the proceedings go ahead there will be a hearing and an affidavit will be sent to you. You can still stop the proceedings but you will need to go to the court to do so. That will happen if you can show that you are in a position to pay, or if your creditor(s) has/have been unreasonable in refusing to accept any offer you may have made. If you want to oppose a Bankruptcy Order, you ought, as a matter of urgency, to ring the National Debtline (0645 500 511). They will be able to

tell you, in layman's language, how you might be able
to do this.

If you are made bankrupt and your debts are less than
£20,000 the court will issue a Certificate of Summary
Administration, which means that the Official Receiver
will be in charge of your affairs.

There are other options. An Administration Order
can be applied if you have at least one county court
judgement against you, and if your total debts do not
exceed the limit of £5000. What this means is that you
make one monthly payment to the county court which
then administers payments to all the creditors on your
behalf. The rules are complicated in the case of secured
debts and joint debts, and some other priority debts, and
you would be very well advised to take advice from
the Citizens Advice Bureau about this very technical
matter.

Or the Official Receiver may accept the option of an
IVA. An IVA does not carry the stigma of bankruptcy,
and if you are subject to one you are permitted to carry
on your business. The IVA may also be tailored to suit
your requirements, just so long as your creditors will
be no worse off than if you were made bankrupt. They
will usually benefit because less money will be spent in
administration than if a bankruptcy results, although the
creditors will have to accept (as in a bankruptcy) that they
cannot expect to receive the full amount of the money due
to them.

There are disadvantages to IVAs. You may have to pay
more, and for longer, than if you become bankrupt. You
will have to use the services of an insolvency practitioner
(a solicitor or an accountant) and they don't come cheap.

For obvious reasons, they will ask for something on account, and that may not be easy to find. What they will do for their money is put together a package offering three quarters of the amount owed to your creditors. The creditors will probably accept this deal because, if they don't, most of your assets will go in administration costs. With an IVA, your home and assets will still be at risk. If the IVA fails to deliver the goods you may still be made bankrupt. Your IVA is recorded in a public register, and this may have an adverse affect on your future credit reference, although not as dismal as if you have been made bankrupt. Once a petition has been received, the proceedings will involve a public examination at which you will be cross-questioned about your financial circumstances.

If you are declared bankrupt, what does that actually mean? Most importantly you will no longer be in charge of your finances. A trustee in bankruptcy will look after all your assets. If you consider him/her as an unpaid financial adviser, you might quite welcome this. You will probably not be allowed to have a bank or building society account, or become or remain director of a limited company, or have more than £250 in credit without telling the creditor about your status as an undischarged bankrupt.

Will you lose your house? Probably. Once you have been made bankrupt, your house will be 'vested' in the Official Receiver, who can only lay claim to your share of the equity. If you can get a consortium of family and friends to chip in and buy out your share, you can remain at home until such time as you can afford to repay them. If your partner and children also live in the house, it's not unusual for you to be allowed a year's grace to find alternative accommodation.

That's the good news. The bad news is that, if the property is mortgaged (and if it isn't why are you thinking of going bankrupt!) you will have to keep up the payments somehow, or the building society, who have prior claims, will take possession – and they *won't* give you a year's grace.

If you're mortgaged to the hilt, there won't be any equity in your property, and the Official Receiver won't take it away from you, though the bank or the building society may!

Even if this happens you ought not to be homeless. The council is obliged to house you, although why and when and how is beyond the scope of this book. Ring the Housing Department which will have the information you need.

Bearing all this in mind, you will not find it easy to carry on a trade or profession, and you may find that trade or professional associations will disqualify you from doing so. You will not be permitted to operate as a magistrate, an MP, a councillor, or an estate agent. You won't be welcome as a solicitor or accountant, or in the civil service, or in a leading security firm. Your house will be at risk, even if you only own a part of it. It is not unknown for the procedures to swallow up all the assets, leaving nothing at all for the creditors. (I once attended a winding-up meeting held against a magazine which owed me £15 for an article I had written about a trip to the Cannes Film Festival. One after another hard-faced creditors stood up to explain that they were owed so many thousands, or tens of thousands, or hundreds of thousands. When I stood up and said: 'What about my fifteen quid?' the meeting collapsed in derisory laughter.)

If you inherit property while the bankruptcy proceedings are continuing, that will become an asset to be distributed. You will almost certainly have to make payments to the trustee of part of your continuing income. And your bankruptcy will have to be advertised in the local paper in case there are outstanding claims by local people.

No, it won't be fun, any more than divorce proceedings are fun, but, as with divorce proceedings, bankruptcy hearings will not last for ever. And if at any time you find yourself in a position to repay the debts and (substantial) bankruptcy expenses in full, or provide full security for them, your Bankruptcy Order can be cancelled. Brilliant.

And always remember that you can only be sent to prison for certain debts (usually non-payment of tax and maintenance payments), and then only if you have the means to pay these and decide that you don't want to. In other words, *you need only go to prison for debt if you choose to.*

Perhaps in concluding this gloomy chapter it might be as well to set out the advantages and disadvantages of Bankruptcy and IVA. Which one you choose ought to depend upon your particular circumstances. Good luck!

BANKRUPTCY

Advantages

1. No more secrecy and deceit.
2. Help from matter-of-fact officials who are used to dealing with such cases.

3. You may not have to pay the full amount owed.
4. The process will only last two years if your debts are less than £20,000 (called a Summary Administration, though it may feel more like a two-year winter). Otherwise three years. But if all your debts are paid in full before the set time, or if you can show that the Bankruptcy Order should never have been imposed, you can apply to have it annulled. After the two or three years you can make a fresh start, and the alternatives may drag on for a good deal longer.
5. You know where you stand and so do your creditors.
6. Once you have been granted a discharge, almost all outstanding amounts will be written off. (The exceptions are secured creditors with security on the home if the home was sold and insufficient raised to settle the debts; fines; maintenance orders; debts from personal injury claims; and any debts incurred through fraud.)

Disadvantages

1. Loss of assets, including any equity in a house or business.
2. Problems of getting credit or a bank account in the future. This may not just be inconvenient, but may adversely affect your earning capacity in the future.
3. The cost. It is likely that more than half of your assets will be used up in the process of going bankrupt.
4. Your affairs will be open to scrutiny.
5. You cannot hold public office, and you may find your employers less than keen to keep you on. Nor can you be a company director without leave of the court.

6. Naturalisation may be made more difficult.
7. Your name will be advertised in the *London Gazette* (if you live in England) and the local press.

IVA

Advantages

1. Not so much bad publicity.
2. If you run a business, you can continue to trade.
3. You may have a say in which assets to hang on to and which to sell.
4. Administration costs are lower than in bankruptcies, and your creditors should get more of what's due to them.
5. The creditors can take no further action against you.

Disadvantages

1. You may have to pay more of your debts.
2. The proceedings will last longer.
3. Your assets will still be at risk.
4. You may still be made bankrupt, if the IVA doesn't work out.
5. Your actions will be closely supervised by the Insolvency Practitioner.

Your status will be recorded in a public register, which will inevitably affect your credit-worthiness.

NOTES ON SCOTTISH PROCEDURE

In Scotland, bankruptcy is known as sequestration. This is a formal process through either the Sheriff Court (for most cases) or the Court of Session. The normal term is three years, at the end of which you are discharged from the debts which you had at the commencement of the sequestration. During this three-year period you are entitled to work and earn a living while making an agreed contribution out of your income to the trustee who is administering your affairs. Any assets which you own are likely to be sold to help to pay your creditors.

A creditor can petition for your bankruptcy or you can present your own petition. He or she must obtain a Court Decree (judgement) for the debt and this must be followed up by issuing a Charge for Payment. If this remains unpaid for fourteen days then the grounds for a Creditor Petition have been established. To commence this procedure the creditor (or it can be a group of creditors) must be owed at least £1500. There are other circumstances where a creditor can raise a petition including where you have signed a trust deed, where you have advised your creditors that you have ceased paying your debts in the ordinary course of business and where there has been a poinding (seizure) of your moveable property and fourteen days have elapsed without payment. A common method is for a creditor to issue a Statutory Demand for Payment of Debt (for at least £1500) to which you must reply within three weeks by recorded delivery to the creditor who sent it. If you do not reply the creditor has established grounds for petition.

Following the petition the court will issue a Warrant to Cite which requires your attendance at court if you wish to dispute the award of sequestration. In your absence, it is likely that sequestration will be awarded against you.

One way to present your own petition is to obtain the concurrence of a qualified creditor. This means a creditor to whom you owe at least £1500, and he must sign your petition application. It is not always easy to obtain this concurrence. The other way in which you can petition is where you have received a Charge for Payment and you have not settled the debt within the fourteen days allowed.

It is possible on occasion to obtain a form of legal aid to pay the solicitor for the petition costs. The costs of the trustee who administers the estate will be met either from the assets which are transferred to him or from government funds (at fixed rates) if the assets are insufficient. If your petition has been properly presented the court must award sequestration.

Both types of petition result in the appointment of a trustee who is responsible for administering your affairs during the three-year period. You will be interviewed by the trustee and you will have to keep him or her advised of any change in your circumstances e.g. change in job or address. At the end of the three-year period you will be automatically discharged from sequestration unless there is reason to believe that there are undisclosed assets.

The sequestration process is administered in Scotland by the Accountant in Bankruptcy, Strategy House, 3 Cables Wynd, Leith, Edinburgh EH6 6DT (Tel: 0131 554 2422). A Bankruptcy Information Pack is available from this source which explains all aspects of the process and advises on how to complete the petition.

12.   Life is Just a Bowl of Cherries

Annual income twenty pounds, annual expenditure nineteen nineteen six, result happiness. Annual income twenty pounds, annual expenditure twenty pounds nought and six, result misery.

> David Copperfield by Charles Dickens
> (Chap. 12, Mr Micawber)

Think back for a moment to one day in your life which you recall as being especially happy. I am prepared to put down good money to wager that it was a day on which you were in a place in which you felt secure and with people you loved. I am further prepared to wager that it was not a day on which you spent enormous sums of money. Picnics. Love-making. Reading an enthralling book. Listening to music. Having a drink or two with a friend. Swimming. Climbing a mountain. Love-making again. Lying in the sun. Playing with your children. An intricate chess match.

Pleasures which, no matter how dire your circumstances, no matter how ominous the future appears, should not be beyond your means. One thing, however, which is absolutely certain is that it will not be easy to enjoy them if you are dreadfully worried about money. Once you have peace of mind, it will not matter if you cannot afford foreign travel. In fact, in most people's

Happiness...

catalogue of their most disastrous experiences it is quite
likely that foreign travel will feature near the top of the
list, just above or just below dying.

I remember an inspiring sermon preached on the morning of the Day of Atonement in a smart synagogue whose
members were well-heeled scions of the Liberal Jewish
community. The timing was intriguing, because earlier
in the week the stock market had fallen further and
faster than anyone could remember. Nobody then knew
how much further it might fall, and it was possible, if
not probable, that some members of the congregation
would be ruined. The rabbi spoke of the events in the
City, but spoke of them as a great blessing, if, as a
result, people were able to achieve a simpler life-style
with more straightforward values.

Did they? I doubt it. But the powerful message that the rabbi passed on came into my mind when I sat down to write what was in danger of being a condescending and sentimental chapter. Back to Basics, was what the Tories called it, but Basics, in their vocabulary meant Opposition.

Peace of mind. Yes, but how? Well, at least, if you agree that that should be your aim, it may help you to employ some of the techniques suggested in this book.

Perhaps what I am arguing for is *realism*. If you take a realistic view as to your current circumstances and your future prospects, what do you see as the most likely outcome of your situation? It is perfectly possible that, if you have been in debt, consistently or sporadically, for several years, and that you are no better off now than you were when you first got into difficulties, you may be living beyond your income. You could be one of those attractive people who, having a rosy picture of how things *could be* and *ought to be*, does not always look too critically at how things *are*. But while you wait for your ship to come sailing into harbour, you are growing older, and the number of years left to you to enjoy peace of mind is diminishing.

If you agree that peace of mind is what you are striving for, what does it really matter if you no longer live in a large house, or even if you own your house? A woman city-dweller told me the other day that she had sold her car because, when she did her sums, she realised that she had paid £1000 in parking fines during the previous year, and that £1000 meant an awful lot of taxi journeys. Simplify.

One of the hardest things to come to terms with is

status. One is reluctant to trade down, because of what people may think. But do you imagine that you will have greater respect from people because of your attempts to live in a manner that it's quite clear you can't afford? And do you imagine that people whose good opinions you care about will think any the less of you, because you no longer live in a big house or drive a shiny car? Children may not like moving to a flat when they are used to living in a house, but they are adaptable, and dislike more than anything not knowing what is going on.

And let us suppose that you take this advice to heart, and, after reading thus far in chapter 12 of this helpful book, you have leapt to your feet, and cried: 'Yes! I shall simplify. I shall move to a cottage. I shall do without a car. I shall live within my means,' that does not preclude you from moving back up to the top of the hill, and buying that snazzy Mazda Mark 5, if and when your ship does come home, as I hope it may.

There are exceptions of course. You may be one of those people who thrives on pressure. I had a friend who was a free-lance writer, and who, having chosen this precarious way of life, had run into debt. His circumstances had put great strain on his marriage, and he would fantasise about how things might change for the better if ever he hit the jackpot. And he did. He wrote a play which was a vast success both here and across the pond, and he made a great deal of money. Lucky fellow. Well, yes, in a way. He paid his debts. He left his wife with a generous settlement with which, I imagine, she was delighted, and probably surprised, to receive. He bought himself a small, but attractive cottage, and installed within it a small but attractive girl friend (had I not mentioned her?). He had one room set aside for his creative work, and arranged for an efficient secretary to come in daily and deal with the boring parts of his career. Then he sat down and waited for inspiration . . . and his mind remained a blank. He thrived on pressure, and now there was none. He has written nothing of note since he became free.

But I believe that for most of us the prospect of organising our lives in such a way that bills can be paid as soon as they come through the letter box (or sooner, if you use direct debit facilities), and we are no longer in dread of the knock on the door, or the hand-delivered letter, and no longer need to invent excuses, is a pleasant prospect, and I believe that if you did not think so too, you would not have read this far through some extremely – I shall be candid – turgid passages.

I hope that that has cleared the air and, if it has, I recommend the following chapter which details some of the ways in which you can have a very good time indeed without spending money you don't have.

13. Living on Air

Boiled cabbage à l'Anglaise is something compared with which steamed coarse newsprint bought from bankrupt Finnish salvage dealers and heated over oil stoves is an exquisite delicacy. Boiled British cabbage is something lower than ex-Army blankets stolen by dispossessed Goanese doss-house-keepers who used them to cover busted-down hen-houses in the slum district of Karachi, found them useless, threw them in anger into the Indus, where they were recovered by convicted beachcombers, with grappling irons, who cut them into strips with shears and stewed them in sheep-dip before they were sold to dying beggars. Boiled cabbage!

from 'Cassandra' by William Connor,
Daily Mirror (1950)

There are books on Indian cookery and Chinese cookery and diet cookery and vegan and vegetarian cookery and microwave cookery and cooking for diabetics. There may well be books on Chinese vegetarian diet-related cookery for diabetics. But what surprisingly there isn't – nothing at least on the shelves of my local public library, which houses a thousand or more books on cookery – is a useful guide to good cooking on a budget, though you may be able to track one down.

Strange. When money is tight there is nothing more satisfying than the ability to continue to provide for

yourself and your family. If you find yourself unemployed, one positive aspect to that worrying condition
is that you do at least have more time to spend on the
preparation of meals, and time properly employed is
more important than money lavishly spent, where home
catering is concerned.

For example: a window box planted with a selection
of herbs is easy and cheap to install and maintain, but
can add sophistication and glamour to the most modest dish.

For example: a jacket potato is a nourishing and
sustaining meal, popular with everyone and capable of
numerous variations.

For example: left-overs are brilliant. Onion skins can
give colour and flavour to stocks and soups. Stalks of

Leftovers ...

cauliflower leaves are delicious cooked in the manner of asparagus.

If left-overs seem inadequate for the number of mouths to be fed, there are a few tricks which can be employed. A large dollop of mashed potato or rice helps to make the meat or fish seem more substantial, especially if you place the meat or fish over the potatoes or rice. Add chopped or sliced hard boiled eggs to poultry and fish in creamy sauces. If there really isn't enough left over to make a main course, turn it into a starter, and then they won't need such a large main course anyway!

Fish is no longer the cheap option it used to be, although whiting, herring and mackerel are not too expensive. Whiting has been thought only suitable for cats, but I find the flavour delicious. Smoked mackerel is especially good value and a bit of a treat when served on toast with a dollop of horseradish sauce. It is also possible to pick up at the big supermarkets packets of smoked salmon offcuts, which taste as luxurious as the real thing, and are brilliant mixed up in scrambled egg. They are not *that* cheap, however.

There are still inexpensive cuts of meat available, including lamb's neck, drumsticks of turkey, knuckle of ham, breast of lamb, pork liver, and lambs' hearts. I include below a recipe for belly of pork, another reasonable option.

Many recipes require the extravagance of butter in the cooking. Use the cheapest brand available for this, but keep a small amount of the best butter for bread, and baked potatoes and things. Olive oil, which is indispensable in many sauces, is an expensive item. The cheapest brand, from Boots the Chemists, lacks flavour, and a better notion is to dilute a good supermarket olive oil with an equal amount of sunflower or groundnut oil.

A cheap or even a halfway decent wine is now cheaper than the equivalent amount of beer. How things have changed in the last two decades! Left-over wine can be preserved longer by pouring a thin layer of olive oil over its surface. Worth doing, because red wine dregs are wonderful for meat stocks, stews, casseroles, and dark sauces, while white wine dregs should be added to fish and vegetable stocks, egg dishes and white sauces. If sherry, port, madeira, vermouth, beer and cider, brandy, or liqueurs are left at the end of a party they should always be used. Find a suitable recipe for whatever you have left by looking up the index of your recipe book.

It's always important to take care over the garnishing of a left-over dish so that, even though you may know its secrets, it will still appear to be something of a treat to the innocents who are about to eat it.

If you have or can afford a freezer, that will facilitate the buying of food in season when it is cheapest, and the cooking of meals in such quantities that what is left may be set aside for future use. Foil, tin foil, cling film, polythene bags and re-usable plastic boxes are essentials, as are adhesive labels and a small notebook detailing not only *what* has been conserved in the freezer but *when* it was put there. Another notebook might be used to jot down recipes which have proved most successful and popular, with a rough guide to how much they cost per head. Even a fridge with a freezer compartment is a great help, although your catering will have to be on a more modest scale.

The other equipment which can pay for itself many

times over before it's clapped out is a food processor, or the cheaper version of a processor, a blender. Soups and sauces and such are marvellously easy if processed or blended; pastry and suet also.

It is always worth making toast in a toaster rather than under the grill. The saving in fuel is considerable, especially if you run to a toaster with an economy setting. Instant coffee has become so expensive that filter coffee made from real beans is a welcome alternative. If you don't have a grinder you can buy coffee already ground. An electric filter coffee-maker is recommended because it is ideal for keeping the coffee hot, or reheating it the following day.

I considered and discarded the idea of providing you with a string of useful recipes, but here are a very few which will give you an idea both of what is possible, and how modest the cost, and although prices will vary locally, the price per portion should not vary that much. All ingredients are for four people.

Potato and Carrot Soup
Less than 20p per portion.

2 large potatoes
4 carrots
2 leeks or 1 large onion
2 pints of water
parsley
knob of butter/ spoonful of oil
small amount of cream (optional) or top of the milk

Cut potatoes into cubes, carrots into slices, and chop onion or leeks. Sweat them in a mixture of a knob of butter and a dessert spoonful of oil with a little salt, for about twenty minutes until softening. Add two pints of water. Bring to the boil, then simmer for about ten minutes until soft. Liquidise. Adjust seasoning. Served with chopped parsley scattered on the top and a little cream or top of the milk.

A hefty slice of bread with the soup will help to fill the crevices.

A Basic Tomato Sauce for Pasta
(one half pint). About 25p per portion.

NB. For a main course allow between 100 and 175 grams (4–6 oz) of pasta per person. And note that cooked pasta will keep 2–3 days if covered and stored in a fridge.

1 large onion
2 cloves garlic
1 tin tomatoes
tomato purée
half a glass of red wine
oregano
basil
1 spoonful of olive oil
1 oz butter
bay leaf
tabasco
salt and pepper

Melt the chopped onion and garlic in equal quantities of oil and butter until they are soft. Add the tomatoes from the tin, the purée, and about half a glass of red wine. Then add the herbs and seasonings and simmer very gently until it has reduced almost to the consistency of jam. Check the seasoning. This sauce may safely be kept in a fridge for up to a week, or in a freezer for three months.

If you can run to fresh pasta, delicious; but dried is quite adequate.

A Basic Vinaigrette
to tart up a tired salad. About 20p per portion.

90 mls (6 tbsp) of olive oil
30 mls (2 tbsp) of wine vinegar
half tsp of caster sugar
half tsp of Dijon mustard
salt and pepper

Put them all in a screw top jar and shake. Before using the vinaigrette give it another shake, and taste it and adjust the seasoning if you need to.

This classic sauce is ideal for all salads, and marvellous poured over large slices of salad tomatoes with a hint of cayenne.

And finally a really substantial and delicious dish, that will not break the bank-manager's heart.

Knuckle of Pork with Boston Baked Beans.
Approximately 85p per portion.

1 pork knuckle
1 lb (450 grams) haricot beans soaked and cooked for an hour
1 tin tomatoes
soy sauce

Worcester sauce
chopped parsley
1 tbsp molasses
3 tbsp honey
1 oz brown sugar
1 tbsp dry mustard
1 tbsp Dijon mustard
2 onions
A spoonful or two of rum
bay leaf, garlic, thyme, salt and pepper

NB If these ingredients sound extravagant, they won't be so if you cook this recipe on several occasions. And you will! However, you could leave out the molasses or the rum.

Put all the ingredients, except the parsley, in a pot and cook them in the oven all day. About an hour before the meal, remove the knuckle, strip off the skin and fat, and remove the bone. Return the chunks of meat to the pot and simmer until required. Garnish with the parsley. Serve with jacket potato and salad. Substantial!

Of course this chapter should include recipes for such marvellous cheap dishes as fish-pie, fish-cakes, shepherd's and cottage pie, rissoles, meat-balls, lasagne and so on, but so long as you check the cost of the ingredients when you make out your shopping list, and work out the approximate cost per portion, you should be able to budget very moderately, especially if you are catering for a large number of eaters. If you can make a chicken or turkey stretch to three meals, it becomes a seriously economical option.

The most extravagant supermarket shopping is the pre-pared meals, and those in which the packaging is more significant than the contents. In an effort to encourage children to eat more vegetables some supermarkets – you'll forgive me if I don't name them here – have been selling shredded vegetables in a child-friendly way, and bumping up the price by a staggering 1000%. Be warned. And take advantage of the welcome policy adopted by many firms of stating the equivalent price per gram, or ounce, of packaged food, to aid comparisons between packets of items and those sold loose. On the other hand special offers of the 'buy two and get one free' variety are often a snare and a delusion, because prices have been raised to make the 'bargain' seem a better deal than it really is.

'Look at all the money we've saved!'

One has to be careful and cute, and, if value and bargains are what you need, the weekly shop cannot be rushed. (On the other hand if you find that you are taking an hour longer on the shop to save £2, and can earn £3 an hour on piece-work done from home, perhaps you should grab what's nearest!)

14. Helpful Hints for Harassed Humans – an Alphabet of Survival

What you are doing is giving your money to somebody else to hold on to, and I think it is worth keeping in mind that the businessmen who run banks are so worried about holding on to things that they put little chains on all their pens.

Henry Beard (1986)

A *APEX* (Advance Purchase Excursion Tickets). Buying airline tickets 1–3 months in advance on scheduled flights may well cut the cost of the ticket in half. Then take out a cheap insurance against being unable to take the flight. You ought *never* to pay the full cost of a flight, and if you decide at the last moment to travel, you can usually get very cheap rates through the newspapers, the Internet, and magazines such as *Private Eye* and *Time Out*. Failing which try to ensure that a member of your immediate family works for the air lines.

B *Banks*. One third of those private customers who go through their bank statements with care find mistakes. You do not need to be clairvoyant to guess that the mistakes are usually in favour of the bank. The best banks appear to be First Direct, Alliance & Leicester, Co-operative Bank, and Royal Bank of Scotland. According to the Consumers Association the worst records are held by Barclays, NatWest, Clydesdale and TSB. The most frequent mistakes were identified as occurring in dealing with direct debits and standing orders, but always take a little time to check your statements and query anything which seems puzzling.

C *Cheque Books.* Apply for replacement cheque books when you don't need them. It is possible to draw out money with the help of a cheque book and a bank guarantee card, but bank clerks have the habit of putting a cross (or other mysterious symbol) against the date on the back inside page of your cheque book when you do this to ensure against you doing it too often.

Clothes. Buying clothes from charity shops is twice blessed. It blesseth him that gives and him that takes. It is also doubly satisfying when you are complimented for the sharpness of your clothes sense to be able to point out that you owe it all to Romanian Orphans. A while ago McDonalds popularised the joke which was then current about how to minimise the cost of your dry cleaning. All you had to do, they said, was take your suit into the charity shop and buy it back the following day, dry-cleaned. The cost of the suit would be less than the conventional dry cleaning bill. For many clothes this is actually and literally true. Charity shops in fashionable areas carry more fashionable clothes but charge more (up to £30 for a man's suit).

The pair of black shoes which I am wearing as I write these words are a bit round-toed for the late nineties, but have leather uppers and have been immaculately maintained. Nor should I worry about the round toes, since I recently spotted a shop specialising in clothes from the seventies and eighties – at prices in excess of even the most ambitious (Oxfam) of the charity shops.

Consumers Association. See entry under *Which?*

Council Tax. If you don't pay this after two reminders, you forfeit the right to pay by instalments, and have to cough up the total amount owing for the year. A nasty shock.

Credit Cards. If you write to your credit card company and threaten to switch to another company unless the annual fee is waived, it is quite likely that you will get a letter back saying that the annual fee has been waived in your exceptional circumstances. Half the sample of Consumer Association members who tried this tactic found it worked. It is, of course, more likely to work if you use your card enough to justify their making the concession.

D *Discounts*. It is not generally known that many quite grand shops, including, I am told, Harrods, are usually prepared to drop the price of their goods by up to 10% for ready cash rather than plastic. Since they have to pay a substantial amount to the credit card company on all the card sales of that company (Amex charges the highest), and have to wait for their money, it's no surprise that they are happy to do this. But since it is improbable that many readers of this book will be Harrods regulars, let me add that the same principle applies in more modest establishments. I have bargained in many shops, often with some effect. My only consistent failure has been in post offices.

E *Ethical Investments and PEPs*. In the unlikely event that you do find yourself with a bit of spare, it is worth pointing out that it has become fashionable (and therefore

profitable) to invest in ethically and environmentally OK
funds. If ever you are in a position to invest, contact EIRIS
(71 Bondway, London, SW8. Tel: 0171 735 1351) for full
details. The opportunity to serve both God and Mammon
comes once in a lifetime!

F *Forgetfulness.* Forget to sign the cheque with which you
pay that desperately overdue bill, especially if you are
expecting a payment in the post. The powers that be
will not cut off your electricity supply if they think that
you have had an attack of absent-mindedness, and by
the time you get the cheque back, pointing out the absent
signature, you may be in a better position to pay it.

G *Gardening.* If you've got a bit of garden, grow vegetables from seed. They cost very little and taste better than

the supermarket vegetables. If you've got a window, use a window box for growing herbs in, and enhance your modest meals with some millionaire flavours.

H *Hairdressing*. Check in the Yellow Pages for the names and addresses of local hairdressers. Many of them are always on the look-out for people to model for them. This means that at the very least you get your hair cut and styled free. Colleges that teach coiffeur are also worth a phone call.

Holiday Brochures. Be canny. Nine out of ten discount offers are not true discounts at all. And check out the possibilities of working holidays. (The local library should be able to direct you to the relevant organisations.) They are often not just affordable, but socially rewarding.

I *Inheritance Tax* (IHT). You are allowed to leave £215,000 each (currently) without having to pay IHT, so it's worth making sure that if one of you is very rich and the other is not you reach an accommodation on behalf of your dependants. Also gifts made at least seven years before the death of the donor are free of IHT. This may not be of much use to you, but if you are likely to inherit it might be worth pointing it out, tactfully, of course, to your living ancestors. Gifts between spouses are free of tax, as are gifts of not more than £3000 a year.

J *Journalism*. There are so many specialist magazines on the newstands that you may well find that any expert knowledge you may have is worth putting into an article and sending to the magazine(s) dealing with such matters. The *Writers and Artists Year Book* is the Bible for details of markets for would-be journalists. Phone the publication first to see if they are looking for free-lance contributions and what they pay.

K *Knitting*. Knit your own clothes. Old magazines, such as are found in Health Centres, have patterns in them. You will have plenty of time to browse.

L *Libraries*. Most public libraries keep a full range of daily and weekly journals and newspapers which may be read on the premises. You may also borrow cassettes and CDs, although a charge is made for these, and you will do better to buy them in the occasional library sales, at charity shops or car boot sales.

M *Modelling*. Art colleges are always in the market for models for life-classes. They prefer models who are not conventionally beautiful. If you *are* conventionally beautiful other – and more lucrative – modelling possibilities may well be available to you.
Mondays. These tend to be half-price days at most cinemas.

N *Naughty but Nice*. Many supermarkets sell fresh cream cakes at a considerable discount towards the end of trading on a Saturday, since the bakery will be shut on the Sunday, and the cakes won't be worth eating on the Monday. Check whether your local supermarket does the same.

O *Opticians*. I discovered, quite by chance, that since my father suffered from cataracts and glaucoma, I was entitled to free eye tests. Indeed this concession applies if any of your close blood relatives has had trouble with their eyes.

P *Parking Fines*. Pay these promptly if you possibly can. In many centres there is now a sneaky device which increases the fine the longer it remains unpaid. The old days when, if you waited long enough you might have acquired diplomatic status, and therefore not have to pay at all, before they caught up with you, are sadly no longer with us.

Petrol. This is usually significantly cheaper if you buy it at your biggest local supermarket.

Q *Queueing*. Many theatres, and concert halls, especially the subsidised ones, invite people to queue for half-price tickets on the evening of the performance – usually from about ninety minutes before curtain up. If the hall isn't full you can always move to best price seats in the interval.

Post-dated cheques. It may seem a sensible idea to suggest paying an overdue bill with a cheque dated at a suitable time in the future when you will have funds available to meet it. Beware. A recent report shows that, through the inattention of bank staff, three-quarters of all post-dated cheques are cashed early.

R *Reward Cards*. These are also known as club cards, promise cards, and suchlike. There is a decided sense of well-being when the check-out person hands you your voucher worth £2.50. Don't be dazzled by the hologram or the impressive graphics. It is a discount equivalent to 1%. Since some big stores are prepared on request to drop their prices by up to 10% for cash, the supermarket concessions are put into perspective. And large signs hanging above tomatoes or cayenne pepper or Weetabix, boasting 'Double Reward on these goods' should be greeted with a sceptical cry of: 'So what else is new?'

S *Second Class Stamps*. There is absolutely no point in sending business letters by first class stamp on a Friday, since they will arrive on a Saturday when the receiving office is shut. It is a serious saving, if you send numerous letters, never to use first class stamps. If you send an enormous number of letters you should buy your stamps from stamp dealers, who are usually willing to sell you current, decimal postage stamps at about 80% of their face value.

T *Telephone Calls*. Take advantage of the cheap rates (mornings, evenings and week-ends) to make all inessential calls. The low-rate scheme instituted by British Telecom for calls made to those whom you call most frequently is substantially worth having. The communications industry is now such a competitive jungle that you would be well advised to shop around anyhow. It may be well worth changing your supplier.

U *Unit Furniture*. Buy a piece at a time, as and when you can afford it and once you have enough you can reassemble it in new and wonderful ways. Try to choose furniture with removable covers, so that the later ones don't make the earlier purchases look shabby. And try to choose a firm that won't go out of business while you are still accumulating.

V *Videos*. If you have a largish family, visits to the cinema can be hellishly expensive. If you wait a few months you can usually hire the film you want to see for £2 or £3, and all see it together. No reason why you shouldn't cook some popcorn for the occasion either. There is a wonderfully cheap cinema in the West End of London, called the Prince Charles (adjoining Leicester Square).

W *Which?* This consumer magazine has done more to raise awareness of cheap-skates and con-men, of sharp practitioners and paperers-over-the-cracks, of sellers-down-the-river and takers-for-a-ride than any number of quangos or well-meaning special committees. Most public libraries carry a complete list of *Which?* magazines, along with the invaluable index, and it is well worth your while if you are contemplating an expensive purchase, or a legal battle, or a house-move or a divorce, or a change to a different bank, or a wedding or a funeral, or almost anything in fact, to trot along and check the appropriate report. The Money section of each edition is printed on green-edged pages, and is invaluable for advice on all such matters, from insurance to investment, from banking to credit cards.

Wills. You ought to make a will but £100 or more is a good deal to pay to a solicitor. There are Do-It–Yourself kits available from stationers, but they have had disastrous consequences. Far better to approach the Consumers Association or the Law Society. A number of firms of solicitors in Scotland and Northern Ireland participate in a Will Aid scheme which encourages you to make a will without having to pay for it. They may be miffed if they are not then invited to administer the estate, but that's their look-out. The Law Society of Scotland will help Scottish inquirers. All these addresses are in Appendix B, of course.

X Vote! for whoever will do most for the poor.

Y *Youth Hostels.* Different youth hostels have different rules about who may and who may not stay at the hostels, for how long, and what the charges are. But it is certainly worth checking them out if you are after an eventful and inexpensive holiday. For details contact: Youth Hostels Association, St Stephens Hill, St Albans, Herts. Tel: 01727 844126.

Z Zzzzzz. Sleep well. You need it.

Appendix A

SOME FURTHER USEFUL INFORMATION

(Readers should be aware that recent devolution votes in Scotland and Wales may lead to changes in some of the following.)

The Bankruptcy Association: 4 Johnson Close, Abraham Heights, Lancaster, Lancs LA1 5EU. Helpline Tel: 01482 658701. (NB This helpline is for members only, but if you ring the helpline it will also tell you how to become a member!

Benefits Agency: Mr P. Mathison, Chief Executive, Quarry House, Quarry Hill, Leeds LS2 7UA. Tel: 0113 232 4000.

The Birmingham Settlement: 318 Summer Lane, Birmingham B19 3RL. Tel: 0121 359 3562. Fax: 0121 359 6357. This is a splendid voluntary organisation, is concerned with Money Advice Training, and runs a series of courses on associated aspects of debt counselling at its Birmingham headquarters. It also produces a useful series of fact sheets, which are short, sensible, and full of the sort of critical information you need to know. The Birmingham Settlement also runs the **National Debtline** (see entry below), a charity providing a telephone answering service on everything you always wanted to know about your debts and were afraid to ask. It is encouraging that this service is currently funded by Natwest UK, TSB Bank plc, Birmingham Midshires, and the Money Advice Trust.

Child Support Agency (CSA) Appeals Tribunal: 8th Floor, Anchorage 2, Anchorage Quay, Salford Quays, M5 2YN. Tel: 0345 626311.

Citizens Advice Bureaux should be your first port of call if you are within easy reach of one. Details are contained within the Yellow Pages, and also within the pages of the Business Sections of the various phone books. Or phone your public libary. The National Association of Citizens Advice Bureaux is at: 115–123 Pentonville Road, London N1 9LZ. Tel: 0171 823 2181.

Companies House (for England and Wales): (postal search) Crown Way, Cardiff CF4 3UZ. Tel: 01222 380801; (for Scotland – postal search) 100–102 George Street, Edinburgh EH2 3DJ. Tel: 0131 225 5774; (for Northern Ireland) Register of Companies, IDB House, 64 Chichester Street, Belfast BT1 4JX. Tel: 01232 234488.

Consumers Association: 2 Marylebone Road, London NW1. Tel: 0171 830 6000. They are on your side.

Consumer Credit Counselling Service: Office Number: 0171 636 5214. Helpline: 0345 697301. This operates a service which reclaims a commission from the creditor for any money it recovers.

Consumer Credit Trade Association: 159 Great Portland Street, W1. Tel: 0171 636 7564. Helpline: 01482 658701. (This helpline is for members only, but if you ring you will be told how to join.)

Council of Mortgage Lenders Arbitration Scheme: 3 Savile Row, London W1. Tel: 0171 437 0655.

Data Protection Registrar: Wycliffe House, Water Lane, Wilmslow, Cheshire SK9 5AF. Tel: 01625 535 777 – for complaints concerning out-of-date or inaccurate personal information held on file.

Department of Social Services Solicitor: New Court, 48 Carey Street, London WC2A 2LS. Tel: 0171 962 8000.

Disability Tribunal: DATs Central Office, PO Box 168, Nottingham NG1 5SX.

Experian: (Formerly CCN, Consumer Help Service) PO Box 40, Nottingham NG7 2SS. Helpline: 0115 941 0888. Experian is a Credit Reference Agency which has issued a book called *Helping You Understand Your Credit File*. This explains what details have been supplied by Experian to mortgage lenders – and what your rights are if the information is incorrect. The other major credit reference company is: **Equifax**, Capital House, 25 Chapel Street, London NW1 5DS. Tel: 0171 298 3000. Also **Equifax Europe UK Ltd**: PO Box 3001, Glasgow G81 2DT. Tel: 01274 759759.

FIMBRA (Financial Intermediaries, Managers and Brokers Regulatory Association): Hertsmere House, Hertsmere Road, London E14 4AB

IMBRO (Investment Management Regulatory Organisation): Broadwalk House, 5 Appold House, London EC2A 2LL. Tel: 0171 628 6022.

Independent Tribunal Services: President HH Judge K. Bassingthwaighte, 4th Floor, Whittington House, 19–30 Alfred Place, WCE1 7LW. Tel: 0171 814 6500. (This office will give details of all regional tribunal services.) In **Scotland** approach: Mrs L.T. Parker, Wellington House, 134–136 Wellington Street, Glasgow, G2 2XL. Tel: 0141 353 1441.

Insolvency Aid: 150 Minories, London EC3. Tel: 0171 264 2099.

The Insolvency Practitioners Association: 119 London Wall, London EC2. Tel: 0171 374 4200 – if you need to talk to someone about liquidators and professional insolvency advice.

Insolvency Service: PO Box 203, 21 Bloomsbury Street, London WC1. Tel: 0171 637 1110.

LAUTRO (Life Assurance and Unit Trust Organisation): Centre Point, 103 New Oxford Street, London WC1A 1QH. Tel: 0171 379 0444.

The Law Society, 113 Chancery Lane, London WC2. Tel 0171 242 1222.

The Law Society of Scotland, 26 Drumsheugh Gdns, Edinburgh 3. Tel: 0131 226 7411. Fax: 0131 225 2934.

National Debtline Tel: 0645 500 511 (local rate number) for information and advice on a person-to-person basis. Monday and Thursday, 10 a.m. – 4 p.m., Tuesday and Wednesday, 10 a.m. – 7 p.m., Friday, 10 a.m. – 12 noon. *Here follow a few locally-based Debtlines. It would be nice to think that by the time this book is published others will be in operation:*

a) **Birmingham:** See under Birmingham Settlement above.

East Sussex: East Sussex Money Advice Direct Debt Line, Southview, Western Road, Hailsham, East Sussex BN27 3DN. Helpline Number: 0345 626 804 (Lo-call). Hours: Weekdays 10 a.m. – 4 p.m. (Wednesdays till 7 p.m.).

b) **Leicester:** City Debtline, Room 4, Town Hall, Leicester LE1 9BE. Helpline: 0116 255 9404. Hours: Tuesdays, Thursdays and Fridays 9.30 a.m. – 12.30 p.m. and 1.30 p.m. – 4 p.m.

c) **London Borough of Croydon:** Croydon Money Advice Helpline, Strand House, Zion Road, Thornton Heath, Surrey CR4 8RG. Tel: 0181 665 5910. Hours: Tuesdays and Thursdays 2 p.m. – 4.30 p.m.

d) **London Borough of Hounslow:** Hounslow Money

Advice Debt Line, 26 Glenhurst Road, Brentford TW8 9BX. Tel: 0181 862 6474. Hours: Tuesdays 2 p.m. – 4 p.m., Thursdays 4 p.m. – 7 p.m.

e) **London Borough of Lewisham:** Mortgage Debtline, Lewisham Money Advice Service, 80 Downham Way, Bromley, Kent BR1 5NX. Tel: 0181 695 9933. Hours: Tuesdays 11 a.m. – 1.30 p.m., Thursdays 1.30 p.m. – 4 p.m.

f) **London Borough of Merton**: Merton Money Advice Service Debt Helpline, 326 London Road, Mitcham, Surrey CR4 3ND. Tel: 0181 640 3194. Hours: Monday 2 p.m. – 4 p.m., Thursdays 10.30 a.m. – 12.30 p.m.

g) **London Borough of Richmond:** Richmond Money Advice Unit Public Advice Line, The Vestry House, 21 Paradise Road, Richmond, Surrey TW9 1SA. Tel: 0181 332 1535. Hours: Tuesday 6 p.m. – 7.30 p.m. Answerphone: 0181 332 7073 – calls will be returned during office hours.

h) **London Borough of Sutton:** Debt Advice Line, Beddington & Wallington CAB, 16 Stanley Park Road, Wallington, Surrey SM6 0EU. Tel: 0181 770 4893. Hours: Wednesday: 2 p.m. – 4 p.m. Answerphone: same number. Can order self-help debt packs outside office hours.

i) **Sheffield:** Sheffield Debtline, 237 London Road, Sheffield S2 4NF. Tel: 0114 255 5455. Hours: Mondays to Fridays 10 a.m. – 4 p.m. Answerphone (same number) allows callers to order self-help booklet outside hours.

Office of Electricity Regulation (OFFER): London Regional Office, 11 Belgrave Road, SW1V. Tel: 0171 233 6366.

Office of Fair Trading: Field House, Bream Buildings, London EC4. Tel: 01781 242 2858 or 0345 224499 (Consumer Information). This is the organisation which regulates the

Consumer Credit Act, covering most loans below £15,000. The office has produced three useful leaflets: *No Credit*, which deals with what credit agencies say about you; *Debt, What to Do When the Bills Pile Up* and *A Buyer's Guide – Your Legal Rights, How to Complain, Where to get Help* (for further useful publications see Appendix B).

Office of Gas Supply (OFFGAS): Stockley House, Wilton Road, SW1. Tel: 0171 828 0898.

Office of Social Security & Child Support Commissioners: Harp House, Farringdon Street, London EC4. Tel: 0171 353 5145; (Scotland) 23 Melville Street, Edinburgh EH3 7PW. Tel: 0131 225 2201.

Office of Telecommunications (OFTEL): 50 Ludgate Hill, London EC4. Tel: 0171 634 8700. Complaints number at local rate: 0345 145 000.

Office of the Rail Regulator: 1 Waterhouse Square, London EC1. Tel: 0171 282 2000.

Office of Water Services (OFFWAT): 15 Ridgemount Street, London WC1 Tel: 0171 636 3656. Complaints number at local rate 0345 581 658. Birmingham Tel: 0121 625 1300.

Ombudsmen:

These are independently appointed Parliamentary Commissioners, appointed to solve disputes. Try them:

Banking Ombudsman: 70 Gray's Inn Road, London WC1. Tel: 0171 404 9944.

Building Societies Ombudsman: Millbank Tower, Millbank, London SW1. Tel: 0171 931 0044.

Corporate Estate Agents Ombudsman: PO Box 1114, 21 Chipper Lane, Salisbury, Wilts. Tel: 01722 333306.

Health Service Ombudsman: Millbank Tower, London SW1 4QP. Tel: 0171 217 4051.

Insurance Ombudsman: City Gate One, 135 Park Street, SE1. Tel: 0171 928 7600.

Investment Ombudsman: 4th Floor, 6 Fredericks Place, London EC2. Tel: 0171 796 3065.

Legal Services Ombudsman: 22 Oxford Court, Oxford Street, Manchester. Tel: 0161 236 9532.

Local Government Ombudsman: 21 Queen Anne's Gate, London SW1. Tel: 0171 915 3210. **Scotland:** 223 Walker Street, Edinburgh EH3 7HX. Tel: 0131 225 5300.   **Wales:** Derwen House, Court Road, Bridgend CF31 1BN. Tel: 01656 661 325.   **Northern Ireland:** Progressive House, 33 Wellington Place, Belfast BT1 6HN. Tel: 01232 233 821.

Parliamentary Ombudsman: Church House, Great Smith Street, London SW1. Tel: 0171 276 2130.

Pensions Ombudsman: 11 Belgrave Road, London SW1. Tel: 834 9144.

Registry of County Court Judgements: Registry Trust Ltd. 173–175 Cleveland Street, London W1P 5PE. Tel: 0171 380 0133. This registers details of all County Court Judgements (CCJs) in England and Wales since 1986, and Scottish decrees and Manx Judgements since 1989. Judgements and administration orders remain on the Register for 6 years, and on your credit reference file until the end of the sixth calendar year. Entries on the Register will be cancelled where an entry was made by mistake, or where a judgement is later set aside. If the judgement is paid in full within one month the court will issue a Certificate of Satisfaction and the County Court Judgement will be shown as satisfied on the Register. Certificates of Satisfaction will be issued after payment of £3 to the court, and after evidence has been produced to show that a judgement debt has been cleared. Members of the public can visit the Registry and for a fee of £4 ask for judgment details of any person by name and address. Postal enquiries cost £4.50 for each name at a specified address.

For the addresses and phone numbers of all **County Courts** (and all other courts as well come to that) see the business phone book for your area – or Yellow Pages or Thomson's Directories.

The Samaritans: 10 The Grove, Slough SL1 1QP. Tel: 01753 532713. Fax: 01753 819004. A splendid, unsentimental organisation. If you ring them about money problems they may refer you to your local **debtline** but will be willing to listen to the ways in which your money problems may be affecting other aspects of your life. They promise complete confidentiality, and their phone lines are staffed by trained volunteers, whose business and practice it is to be sympathetic and discreet. Check local phone books for local numbers. Telephone calls to the Samaritans are free.

Solicitor's Complaints Bureau: Portland House, Stag Place, London SW1E 5BL. Tel: 0171 834 2288.

Appendix B

SOME FURTHER USEFUL READING

The government inspired leaflets referred to throughout the text may be found in Post Offices, Public Libraries,

Council Offices, Citizens Advice Bureaux, and so on. Here are a few more books which I have found to contain information not always available elsewhere. You should find all of them in your local public library; if not, write to the publishers or charity responsible.

The daddy of them all is the *Catalogue of all Social Security Leaflets* (CAT1), available free from Her Majesty's Stationery Office, The Causeway, Oldham Broadway Business Park, Chadderton, Oldham OL9 OX9.

I have referred elsewhere to the brilliant leaflets published by the **National Debtline**. Write to them at the Birmingham Settlement, 318 Summer Lane, Birmingham, B19 3RL or ring them on 0645 500 511 for an update on their latest publications. Already available are:

Dealing with your Debts (Mortgage Pack) £5.00
Dealing with your Debts (Rent Pack) £5.00
Full Set of Fact Sheets £12
Individual Fact Sheets 75p (but minimum order £1.50)

I hope you won't need *A Guide to Bankruptcy*, published free by the DTI's Insolvency Service (for details see Appendix A). But if you need it, you do need it!

Excellent books are published by the **Child Poverty Action Group**, 1–5 Bath Street, London EC1V 9PY. Don't be put off by the unsexy titles. Recommended ones are:

National Welfare Benefits Handbook (income-related benefits) £8.95 or £3 to benefit claimants.
Rights Guide to Non-Means-Tested Social Security Benefits £8.95 or £3 to benefit claimants.

Jobseekers' Allowance Handbook £6.95 or £2.50 to benefit claimants.

Then there's **CHAR**, the housing campaign for single people at 5 Cromer Street, London WC1. Tel: 0171 833 2071. They publish annually:

The Benefits Guide £7.95. Very detailed and a well signposted path through a murky forest.
Young People – The Children's Act and Homeless 16 and 17 Year Olds £7.50
Community Care £4.70.

Age Concern Astral House, 1268 London Road, London SW16 4ER. Tel: 0181 679 8000 publishes:

Your Rights 1997–1998 (benefits for older people) £3.99.
Money Matters – Your Taxes and Savings 1997–1998 £4.95.
Using Your Home as Capital 1997–1998 £4.95.
The Pensions Handbook 1997–1998: a mid-career guide to improving retirement income, £6.95.
Changing Directions: Employment Options in Mid-Life £6.95.
Your Retirement £4.95.
Healthy Eating on a Budget £6.95.
Housing Options for Older People £4.95.

The Disability Alliance, 1st Floor East, Universal House, 88–94 Wentworth Street, London E1 7SA. Tel: 0171 247 8776. Fax: 0171 247 8765 is responsible for *Disability Rights Handbook* £10.50 (or £6.50 if receiving any state benefit).